THERE'S ONLY ONE
SAUZÉE

ALSO BY TED BRACK

There is a Bonny Fitba Team: Fifty Years on the Hibee Highway

Pat Stanton's Hibernian Dream Team
(Pat Stanton with Ted Brack)

The Life and Times of Last Minute Reilly
(Lawrie Reilly with Ted Brack)

THERE'S ONLY ONE SAUZÉE

When Le God Graced Easter Road

TED BRACK

BLACK & WHITE PUBLISHING

First published 2011
by Black & White Publishing Ltd
29 Ocean Drive, Edinburgh EH6 6JL

1 3 5 7 9 10 8 6 4 2   11 12 13 14

ISBN: 978 1 84502 350 8

Typeset by RefineCatch Ltd, Bungay, Suffolk
Printed and bound by ScandBook AB, Sweden

CONTENTS

ACKNOWLEDGEMENTS

TOWARDS the end of 2010, I attended a family engagement party. I had just written my third book on Hibs and was starting to weigh up options for my next. During the evening, my nephew Nick Dishon and his friends Bruce Brown and Colin Smith approached me. They too were interested in what I was going to do next. In fact, they had given the matter some consideration. They pointed out that my previous books had dealt with Hibs in eras before they were born and told me that it was time I turned my hand to something more up to date. Indeed, Bruce had a suggestion to make. He asked me what I thought about producing an account of Franck Sauzée's time at Easter Road.

I thought it was a great idea and in the days that followed, I canvassed opinion from Hibs friends and acquaintances young and old. They were all equally enthusiastic, so the concept of *There's Only One Sauzée* was born.

Writing the book has been a real pleasure and not least because of the support I have received from so many football people. I want to thank Alex McLeish for his excellent foreword and for sharing his memories of his time as Hibs manager with me. Former chairman Malcolm McPherson was honest and helpful and provided me with valuable background information for the book.

Franck Sauzée's ex-team mates Ian Murray, Stuart Lovell, John O'Neil and Nick Colgan all spoke freely to me and made clear their love of Hibs in the process. A number of former players from earlier eras also provided me with much appreciated thoughts on the influence of Franck Sauzée. The book was enhanced too by excellent contributions from media people like David Hardie, Chick Young, Richard Gordon, Simon Pia and Grant Stott.

My former colleagues from the *Hibs Monthly* fanzine, Stevie Burns, Sandy Mcnair, Colin Leslie, Sean Allan and John Campbell, have also enriched the Sauzée story with their thoughts and recollections. The fanzine was popular and provocative in the days before Internet websites took precedence and the quality of writing it contained has been confirmed by the fact that several of its former contributors are now authors in their own right.

Franck Sauzée loved the Hibs supporters and they revered him in return, so I wanted to give the fans a voice in this book. I want to record my appreciation of all the Hibs supporters who provided me with memories for the book's final chapter. One of these Hibees, Sean McPartlin, has the distinction of having visited Franck Sauzée's hometown of Aubenas. Another, Derek Emslie, was able to provide insight on Franck the man as well as Franck the footballer.

Fife Hyland and everyone at Hibernian Football Club have been tremendously helpful with all of my Hibs books and that has been the case again with *There's only One Sauzée*. My thanks to them. The Hibernian match day programmes from the Sauzée era have been a most helpful source for my research. They were of high quality back then and they still are today.

As always, I want to thank my close family. My wife Margaret, daughter Lisa and sons Patrick, Dominic and Kevin have all given me constructive feedback, which has made the final version of the book better than it otherwise would have been.

I also want to say a heartfelt thank you to Campbell Brown, Alison McBride, Janne Moller, John Richardson, Rachel Kuck and Paul Eckersley at Black & White Publishing for their support with producing the book.

Then, there's Monsieur Sauzée himself. A personal input from Franck would have put the icing on the cake as far as the book was concerned. As you will see from the postscript at the end of the book, with help from a lot of people, I made strenuous attempts to contact him and involve him in my project. Despite my best efforts, I didn't manage to make personal contact with Franck. He guards his privacy jealously and, in the end, I had to respect that. This book, then, is not an authorised biography. It is simply my account of the pleasure and the glory that Franck Sauzée brought to all Hibs supporters during his time at Easter Road.

I hope you enjoy the book as much as I enjoyed watching Franck strut his stuff.

Ted Brack

FOREWORD

BY ALEX MCLEISH

IN FEBRUARY 1999, Hibernian were well on their way to winning the Scottish First Division Championship and returning to where they belonged in the top flight of Scottish football. My thoughts, as manager of the club at that time, were not just on securing promotion. I was also looking ahead to our return to the SPL.

When I heard that Franck Sauzée might be available, I was immediately interested. I knew the world game well and was aware of Franck's ability and status. I had also played against him in international football and had no doubt that Franck could make a significant difference to Hibs in the seasons ahead.

As everyone now knows, I was able to persuade Franck to sign for Hibs. I made him aware of the club's history and traditions and stressed to him the great potential that existed at Easter Road. I also told him that the club's supporters expected their team to play with flair and style. He liked that.

Franck began his Hibernian career as a midfield player. His ball control and passing, both short and long, were outstanding. Although a highly skilled footballer, he was also strong in the tackle. He had a terrific shot in him too and he gave us goals both in open play and from dead ball situations. Most of all, though, Franck was a role model and inspiration to the other players. He led by example and gave his team mates self belief by doing so.

At the beginning of season 2000–2001, I moved Franck to sweeper. I wanted him to use his ability to read the game to keep us secure in defence and to initiate attacks from the back. I believed that Franck was capable of making us stronger defensively while adding to our creativity at the same time. I was proved absolutely correct. Franck, and Hibs, had a great season. We beat Hearts 6–2 and reached the Scottish Cup Final against Celtic, and Franck was instrumental in much of our success.

When I left Hibs, Franck succeeded me as manager. His tenure of the manager's chair was to be brief. Franck was only in the job for sixty-nine days, so it is impossible to make any informed judgements on his managerial capabilities.

We can most certainly judge him as a person and as a footballer, though. He is a fine man. He is pleasant and friendly and laid back by nature. Don't let that fool you, however. Like all great players, Franck has a true winner's mentality. Make no mistake about it either, Franck Sauzée was a truly great player. His achievements for Marseille, his other clubs and for his country, France, speak for themselves.

However, this book is about Franck's time at Hibernian. The Hibs fans took to him immediately. They revered his talent and saw that he shared their affection for their club. Two things sealed the great bond between Franck Sauzée and all followers of Hibs. The supporters loved his classy, commanding play, but most of all they knew that this man respected their team and knew exactly how much it meant to them as fans. That was because it meant just as much to him as a player.

I am proud to have brought Franck Sauzée to Hibs. I am proud, too, of what the club achieved during my time in charge. We progressed from being a First Division team to a side that played free-flowing, attacking football, reached a cup final and qualified for Europe in a pleasingly short space of time. Franck Sauzée was at the forefront of this successful period in Hibs history.

Franck formed a very special relationship with the Hibs support that survives to this day. It is only right that his contribution to

Hibernian Football Club should be fully recognised. That is why I welcome the publication of *There's Only One Sauzée*. Ted Brack's account of Franck Sauzée's time at Hibs will recall very happy times for all those who follow the fortunes of the Hibees.

I, too, have many fond memories of my time at Easter Road. My brother is married to an Edinburgh girl who is a faithful Hibs fan, so there is a strong McLeish family Hibernian connection. This record of the Sauzée years at Hibs, which also happened to be the McLeish years, has brought back to me memorable events such as our runaway promotion campaign, the derby victories, the Scottish Cup runs in both 2000 and 2001, and that great European night when AEK Athens came to Easter Road.

Enjoy the book.

Alex McLeish

INTRODUCTION

THE SIGNING OF A SUPER STAR
CALLED SAUZÉE

HIBERNIAN FOOTBALL CLUB has a long and illustrious history. Founded in 1875 by Canon Edward Hannan, the parish priest of St Patrick's Church in Edinburgh's Cowgate, in partnership with his immigrant Irish parishioners, Hibs soon began to make a name for themselves in Scottish football.

In 1887, they won the Scottish Cup for the first time and later that year, they defeated England's then top team Preston North End to become unofficial Champions of the World. In 1902, they won the Scottish Cup for a second time after defeating Celtic, who, after their formation in 1888 with tremendous support from Hibs, had repaid this kindness by repeatedly signing the club's best players (a practice which continues to this day). Unbelievably, this splendid trophy has not been lifted by a Hibs captain since. Almost 110 years have passed since the Scottish Cup was bedecked in the green and white ribbons of Hibernian and Hibs supporters, while wanting desperately to witness this piece of silverware being captured again, have long since resigned themselves to never seeing it happen.

Hibs ceased playing in 1891 in order to sort out their finances and find a new ground, but returned to the fray in 1893. In 1990, the club fought for its future once more as the chairman of Heart of Midlothian, Wallace Mercer, launched a hostile takeover bid for Hibs. Thanks to the efforts of the Hands off Hibs group – led by the late, great Kenny McLean – and the intervention of Tom Farmer, Hibs survived.

Between these two flirtations with extinction, Hibernian earned a reputation for fast, free-flowing football. This style of play was best epitomised by the great Hibs side of the late 1940s and early 1950s. Inspired by its Famous Five forward line, this team won the Scottish League Championship three times in five years and reached the semi-final of the inaugural European Cup. They also blazed the trail in floodlit football and travelled all over the world to meet (and very often beat) the best clubs in Europe and South America.

In the 1960s, Hibs defeated Barcelona and Real Madrid and in the following decade, the great Turnbull's Tornadoes team, managed by former player Eddie Turnbull and captained by all-time Easter Road great Pat Stanton, won one League Cup and two Drybrough Cups.

The seventies ended on a low note, though, when Hibs were relegated. They returned to the top league at the first time of asking and, after the Mercer takeover had been successfully resisted, captured the League Cup again in 1991. Only seven short years after this glorious and emotional triumph, however, the mighty Hibernian once again found themselves in the First Division.

This ignominy was not well received by the club's fans but one thing that can never be denied is the loyalty of the Hibernian support. When season 1998–99 got underway, Hibs followers turned out in numbers to cheer their team back to the top league. Initially, the cheers turned to jeers as Hibs lost to Stranraer and St Mirren and drew with Clydebank, but as manager Alex McLeish, with the backing of a supportive board of directors, began to strengthen his team, results started to improve.

First, McLeish signed Mixu Paatelainen from Wolverhampton Wanderers. The big centre forward brought experience and confidence to go with his undoubted ability. He began to score goals and brought out the best in those around him.

Next came a masterstroke. Hibs Trinidadian winger Tony

Rougier, whose great skills were often rendered ineffective by an attitude that his proponents described as laid back and his detractors called lazy, was on his way out of Easter Road as the club had accepted an offer for his services from Port Vale.

Before he left, Tony mentioned casually to his manager that one of his international colleagues, Russell Latapy, had become disenchanted with life at Boavista in Portugal and might be available on a free transfer. Latapy had also played for Porto. Indeed, he had reached the European Cup semi-final with them.

Porto are famous now for having won the Champions League under Jose Mourinho but they were managed by another of football's greatest managers before Mourinho came to the fore. Bobby Robson had occupied the managerial hot seat at Porto after leading England to the 1990 World Cup semi-final and it was to the great Geordie that McLeish turned when he wanted to check out Latapy's pedigree.

In his inimitable way, Robson responded to McLeish's enquiries by saying, 'The boy Latapy? Aye, a good little player.' Russell was duly contacted and invited to Scotland for a trial. Aston Villa and Ipswich Town were also showing an interest in acquiring his services, so Hibs didn't have time to waste.

Rightly though, McLeish wanted to see Latapy play for himself, so he arranged a friendly match at Brechin. It is a tribute to the manager's powers of persuasion that he was able to get Russell to agree to come. The match took place on an inhospitable evening at Glebe Park but Hibs Trinidadian trialist illuminated his mundane surroundings. After five minutes of play, McLeish and his assistant Andy Watson exchanged knowing looks. They had seen enough. They knew they had found a little gem.

Their next task was to see off the competition from down South and persuade Latapy to put pen to paper on a contract at Easter Road. To their great credit, they did exactly that. When asked years later what he had thought of his first sight of Scotland and in particular of Brechin, Russell Latapy replied, 'It was cold man, very, very cold.'

But the Scottish climate didn't deter the little magician from committing himself to Hibs and soon his play-making skills were inspiring his new team to go on a long unbeaten run. The festive period was particularly fruitful as large crowds packed Easter Road to see Ayr United and Raith Rovers put to the sword.

It was clear by this point that the destination of the First Division Championship would be determined by a confrontation between Hibs and Falkirk. The Brockville club, as they were then, had a team packed full of experience and fight and their compact old ground, although showing its age in its state of repair, was full of atmosphere and intimidating to opposing teams.

Hibs were due to travel to Falkirk in February 1999 for a match that promised to go a long way towards deciding the outcome of the championship. McLeish's team was much improved from its early season travails but it was still some way removed from being the finished article.

As the club's supporters looked ahead to the forthcoming weekend visit to Brockville and viewed the prospect with no little trepidation, rumours that were bordering on the incredible began to sweep through Edinburgh. The word on the streets was that Hibs were trying to sign Franck Sauzée.

Hibs fans were not unused to wild and unfounded speculation. In the 1980s, a rumour had gone round the ground during a New Year derby match that Rod Stewart had bought Hibs. Sadly, he hadn't and most Hibs supporters expected this latest piece of optimistic gossip to come to a similarly unfulfilled conclusion.

However, the story began to gain credence and it took a step further when newspaper reports confirmed that Alex McLeish was indeed in talks with Sauzée. This was amazing. Sauzée had had a sparkling career at both club and international level and had won more than his fair share of glittering prizes. Only six years previously, he had been one of Marseille's star players as they had lifted the Champions League. Now, Franck was with Montpellier and, so it seemed, seriously considering making a move to Easter Road.

This was potentially Hibs' most sensational signing since George Best had joined the club twenty years earlier. Best, magnificently talented though he still was, had been struggling to find a club due to his extra-curricular activities and had been enticed to Easter Road by the promise of big money payments for every game he played from Hibs' then chairman Tom Hart. This was not the case with Sauzée, who was well known for his healthy lifestyle and dedication to fitness.

The word legend is undoubtedly overused in football these days but, in the case of Franck Sauzée, the term was totally appropriate and fully merited. The French genius, born in the village of Aubenas in the Ardeche, was a genuine soccer super star, so why was he considering moving to Hibs?

There were a number of reasons. Sauzée's coach at Montpellier was young and worried about his job. He saw the great man as a threat and, putting his personal position before the good of his team, kept him at arm's length. Communication between the two had completely broken down and the Montpellier coach was happy to present Sauzée to his club as an older player who was past his best and should be allowed to move on. This coach's insecurity and fear for his own future was to do Hibs a very great favour indeed.

Another factor in making this most unlikely of transfer deals a very real possibility was the standing of Hibs' manager in world football. Alex McLeish had played against Franck Sauzée in World Cup matches. They knew, liked and respected each other, so when McLeish made his initial call to Montpellier, Sauzée was prepared to listen.

The great man was now thirty-three years old and, because of a lack of recent match play, a little short of full fitness. McLeish asked him if he would come to Edinburgh and play in a closed-doors match. This was a bit like asking Luciano Pavarotti to perform at a concert in Leith Town Hall to see if his vocal chords were still capable of making melodic sounds but, being both a modest man and one of nature's gentlemen, Sauzée agreed.

Over to Edinburgh he came and he took part in a bounce game. In the first half he played at sweeper and in the second half he occupied a midfield role. McLeish and Watson could see that, while Franck needed match practice to fully restore his fitness, his array of footballing skills was undiminished. They decided that if he played in midfield with Latapy, then these two soccer classicists could show their colleagues the value of composure, playing with the head up and retaining possession. They could also bring incisive passing and goals to the party and help Hibs make the transition from an improving team to a side worthy of competing in the higher echelons of the top division once again.

The next step was to persuade Sauzée to uproot himself and come to Easter Road. McLeish extolled the virtues of Edinburgh as a city to live in and made it clear that Hibs were a great club that had temporarily fallen on hard times. He assured the French master that a return to the big time was just around the corner and that he could play a major part in achieving this. The board weighed in with a healthy wage offer, which did no harm either, and a couple of days before the crucial trip to Brockville, Franck Sauzée shocked the footballing world and rendered all Hibs supporters ecstatic by signing for Hibernian Football Club.

Falkirk's dilapidated but cacophonous old ground was full for this vital match. The old terracing space behind one goal was closed for safety reasons but the rest of the stadium, including the venerable main stand, was bursting at the seams. Thousands of Hibs supporters had made the journey for a game that would go a long way towards deciding whether their club could make an immediate return to the SPL. They were there too, of course, to welcome a Gallic Great to the Hibernian Family. The home team was not short of support either and their fans were as hostile to their visitors as they were raucous in their backing for their own team.

Three minutes before three o'clock on a very wet, windy and cold Saturday, 20 February 1999, Franck Sauzée took the field for the first time as a Hibs player. He received the warmest of welcomes from the travelling Hibs support, most of whom, in truth, could hardly believe what was in front of their eyes.

Wearing the number eight jersey, a pair of black gloves to keep out the rigours of the Scottish winter and positively glowing with health, Sauzée embarked on his Hibs career. He must have found his baptism to be of a very fiery nature indeed. On a tight pitch and muddy surface, the game was played to a backdrop of deafening noise as the two teams fought for supremacy.

The Falkirk side was full of players who had been around and knew how to use their experience to the best advantage. They were Hibs' main challengers for promotion and every bit as keen to return to the top flight. They went at Hibs with gusto from the first whistle but McLeish's men were made of stern stuff and withstood all that was thrown at them.

As half time approached, Hibs took the lead. Little Latapy rose above the mayhem around him to pick out a slide rule pass that sent Paul Hartley through. Hartley displayed admirable coolness to stay onside and slot the ball past Paul Mather in the Falkirk goal. At this stage of his career, Hartley was a tricky winger. No one would have suspected at that time that he would re-invent himself as a midfield player who enjoyed great success with Hearts, Celtic and Scotland, and inflicted a lot of pain on Hibs in the process. For the moment though, Hartley was a Hibee and his goal took his team into the half time interval with a welcome lead.

The referee at Brockville this day was Kevin Toner. Toner's father Willie had once played for Hibs but on this occasion, his son was showing no sign of any warm feelings towards his father's former team. Toner first sent off Paul Hartley. He then proceeded to award Falkirk a number of questionable free kicks on the edge of the Hibs penalty area. From one of these free kicks, Oli Gottskalksson could only parry Scott Crabbe's shot and Marino Keith pounced on the rebound to fire Falkirk level.

The ten-man Hibs side were now fighting for their lives and their hopes of becoming First Division Champions at the end of the season were on a knife edge. At this point, Franck Sauzée took a hand. As this fast and furious match had raged around him, Sauzée had made the occasional deft intervention. Indeed, at one point, he had indulged in a bit of keepie uppie as he had carried the ball forward into the Falkirk half. In truth, though, due to his lack of recent match practice, Franck had been peripheral in the game. This was to change. As the second half wore on, Sauzée made a crucial contribution. He moved across the field with the ball and, while looking in one direction, back heeled the ball into the space behind him. Right back Derek Collins fastened on to this exquisite touch and shot for goal. His shot took a significant deflection and looped into the Falkirk net. This goal won the match and played a vital part in ensuring that Hibs stayed on course to be First Division Champions.

At full time, the Hibs support acclaimed their team, who had done something that Hibs sides are not famed for; they had shown strength in the face of adversity. Among the applause and cheers, a song began to go up. The fans were singing 'Sauzée, there's only one Sauzée'. Out on the pitch, Franck took time to assimilate what he was hearing. He then broke into a grin and clapped his hands above his head. A love affair between Franck Sauzée and the Hibs support, which was mutual in its intensity, had begun. An exciting chapter in the history of Hibernian Football Club was about to be written.

1

THE MAKING OF A FRENCH
FOOTBALL LEGEND

THIS BOOK is about the time Franck Sauzée spent at Hibs as a player and a manager. Most Hibs fans, those who were privileged to see Franck play in the green and white and those who, through age, have had to make do with stories from older family members about how great a player he was, probably don't know all the details of Sauzée's illustrious career before he came to Easter Road.

It is quite some time now since Le God played his last game for Hibs. That means that younger Hibs supporters either never saw Franck play at all or saw him at an age when they were too young to fully appreciate just how special a performer they were watching. Those who are that little bit older, or indeed much older, will know full well that Franck Sauzée's spell with Hibs was one of the better times in the club's history and something to be treasured.

All followers of Hibs at the time were aware that when Alex McLeish brought Franck Sauzée to Hibs, he was recruiting a player of high quality. They knew the main details of Franck's career before he joined Hibs. Most of them, though, didn't realise just how successful and distinguished that career had been.

The purpose of this short opening chapter is to set the scene for what follows. It is important that all readers of this book, most of whom will probably be of a Hibernian persuasion, enter the main part of it fully conversant with the magnitude of the coup that Franck Sauzée's signing by Hibs represented. This was not just a good player or even a very good player coming to Easter Road late in his career, this was a truly great player.

Franck Sauzée was born in Aubenas in the Ardeche area of Southern France on 28 October 1965. This was a time when Harold Wilson was getting to grips with becoming Great Britain's first Labour Prime Minister for thirteen years, The Beatles, Rolling Stones and Bob Dylan were composing and performing ground breaking music on what seemed like a weekly basis and Hibs were coming to terms with the shock loss of their manager Jock Stein.

Stein had left Hibs in the spring of 1965 to return to his first love, Celtic. When he left, Hibs were very well placed to win both the Scottish League and the Scottish Cup. In the event, demoralised by their inspiring leader's departure, the players lost their way and the season ended in bitter anti-climax.

The man charged with the daunting task of replacing Stein was Bob Shankly. The brother of Liverpool's flamboyant 'Shanks', Bob Shankly was a quiet man who knew the game inside out. He had already won the league and done well in the European Cup with Dundee before coming to Easter Road. He had clearly made a good start with Hibs, as just a few weeks before Franck Sauzée's birth, he led the team to Tynecastle and saw them beat Hearts 4–0 with all the goals, which were equally shared between Eric Stevenson and Jimmy O'Rourke, being scored in the first ten minutes. It is interesting to reflect now that just a few months after one influential Hibernian figure in Jock Stein left Easter Road, another of the club's great names, in the shape of Franck Sauzée, was coming into the world.

If you look up Aubenas on the Internet, you will see that these days it is best known for commerce, tourism and the production of the type of food that is stocked by delicatessens. The web-based information also contains a list of Aubenas' most famous citizens, past and present. This list includes politicians, priests, historians, journalists and sportsmen. The sporting heroes are made up of an athlete, a handballer, a rugby player and several footballers. With one exception, none of the names are of the household variety and, it is very clear, one of the football players stands head and shoulders above the rest as Aubenas' most celebrated sporting son. That man of course is Franck Sauzée. If Hoboken did the rest of the planet a great favour when it exported Frank Sinatra, Aubenas gladdened the heart of the footballing world when it produced its very own Franck in the shape of Sauzée.

Franck's dad was a keen amateur footballer and he and his wife gave their son great encouragement as he began to develop his talent for football. It didn't take long for this talent to be recognised and for the seventeen-year-old Sauzée to be snapped up by Sochaux.

Franck was still a couple of months short of his eighteenth birthday when he made his league debut against FC Rouen in August 1983. He was soon an established first team player and, very obviously, a player with a major future, as he earned rave reviews on a regular basis. At the end of the 1986–87 season, Sochaux were relegated but in a reflection of the situation that Franck was to experience with Hibs twelve years later, they used this setback to positive effect. They won promotion in their first season and managed to reach the French Cup Final while doing this.

Sadly, Sochaux lost to Metz on penalties but they had returned to the top flight in a much healthier state than they had left it. However, they would have to face their return to football at the highest level without their great young player. In 1988, Franck Sauzée moved to Olympique Marseille. He left behind him at Sochaux a most impressive record for a midfield player of forty goals in 150 matches. One of his team mates had been worthy of the description 'impressive' as well, because, while at Sochaux, Franck had played beside the one and only Eric Cantona.

Sauzée had also been a member of the French under-21 team that had won the European Championships in 1988 and, in the August of that same year, he had made his full international debut in a friendly match against Czechoslovakia in Paris. Franck was rarely to miss a match for his country after that until he decided to retire from international football in 1993.

The move to Marseille was hugely successful. The club won the league in both season 1988–89 and season 1989–90. They also won the Coupe de France for good measure in 1989. During these successful campaigns, Franck Sauzée played sixty-eight games and scored nine goals. He was earning a reputation as one of the best midfield players in Europe and compiling quite a collection of trophies and medals.

However, he was on the move again in the summer of 1990, transferring his allegiance on this occasion to Monaco, who were under the expert stewardship of Arsene Wenger. The combination of the deep thinking, master strategist Wenger and the dynamic, highly skilled Sauzée looked like a footballing match-up made in heaven and so it proved. Monaco won the French Cup in 1991 and their successful season was spearheaded by Sauzée, who notched up seven goals in twenty-eight appearances. Meanwhile, in Sauzée's absence, Marseille had reached the 1991 European Cup Final only to lose on penalty kicks to Red Star Belgrade.

Sauzée was surely enjoying playing for Wenger. He was undoubtedly benefitting from the experience. Nonetheless, when the call to go back to the Stade Vélodrome came, Franck answered in the affirmative. His return was to prove pivotal in Marseille, at last winning European club football's premier trophy, becoming the first, and to date only, French team to lift that trophy in the process. By the time Sauzée rejoined Marseille, he had captained his country and scored goals for his national team as well, so his reputation continued to grow.

Marseille had won the French league again in 1991–92 and this entitled them to compete in the following season's UEFA Champions League, as the European Cup was now known. This time they went all the way, lifting the famous trophy, first claimed by Real Madrid in 1956, by beating AC Milan 1–0 in Munich in the final. A key group match en route to the final had been against Glasgow Rangers. Rangers were, at that time, awash with money and big names, and thus posed a genuine threat. However, a superb strike by none other than Franck Sauzée ensured that the French team, rather than the Scots, progressed to the ultimate stage of the competition.

Sauzée treasured the famous triumph in Munich. He said, 'It was a special time. There was a great bond between the fans and the team. Because we were the first French team to win the trophy, the whole country was behind us.'

Marseille won the league again in 1993 but at that point, a scandal emerged. The club's president, Bernard Tapie, was found to have bribed one of Marseille's opponents during their league campaign. The club was immediately stripped of the 1992–93 league title. It was also banned from defending the Champions League the next season.

Franck Sauzée had this to say about Tapie – 'Every day with him was not easy but he became a big figure in the club's history.'

Sadly for Olympique Marseille's devoted fans, their great team began to break up in the wake of the bribery scandal. A side which, at different stages, had contained such great players as Sauzée, Didier Deschamps, Alen Boksic, Jean-Pierre Papin, Chris Waddle and Marcel Dessailly, splintered and the players who had become the heroes of the Vélodrome dispersed to seek their footballing fortunes elsewhere.

In that same year of 1993, Franck Sauzée called time on his international career. He had played for France on thirty-nine occasions and scored nine goals. He had captained his country on nine occasions. His last match was the infamous World Cup qualifying match against Bulgaria at the Parc des Princes.

A draw would have been sufficient for France to qualify for the 1994 Finals in the USA and they were comfortable at 1–1. At that point, the highly talented David Ginola had the chance to pick out Eric Cantona for what would have been a second and probably decisive French goal. Ginola misdirected his pass. The Bulgarians gained possession and went up the other end and scored. This goal was enough to win them the match and knock France out of the

World Cup. The scorer was Emil Kostadinov, who curiously enough, Alex McLeish was identifying as a possible signing target for Hibs at the same time as he was considering a move for Franck Sauzée.

Ginola was castigated for his error and given a hard time by fans across France on his return to club football. The talented winger was so upset by some of the comments made by his national manager Gerard Houllier that he considered taking legal action. He opted instead to move to England where he carved out a successful career with Newcastle United, Tottenham Hotspur, Aston Villa and Everton.

Houllier had replaced Michel Platini as manager of France and this change at the top of French football may have had something to do with Franck Sauzée's decision to give up playing for his national team. Sauzée is on record as saying, 'I was tired of playing for the French team. If you don't feel right, you can't carry on. When Platini left, I was very disappointed and I didn't have the same enthusiasm.'

Whatever his reason for giving up international football at the age of twenty-eight, Franck Sauzée never returned to play for his country again, which makes his final record on the international stage all the more impressive.

Interestingly, as one great player left the French fold, another entered it. In August 1994, Zinedine Zidane made his full inter-national debut. He and Sauzée missed each other by months. What a combination they would have made if they had played together.

Serie A in Italy had a high profile in the 1990s and Atalanta was Franck's next port of call. It wasn't to prove a happy destination. The club coach, Francesco Guidolin, was sacked only ten games into the season and the club ended up being relegated. Bizarrely, Franck Sauzée, in his prime as a footballer, made only sixteen starts and managed just one goal. The club finished second from bottom of the league and was demoted to Serie B. At that point, Franck Sauzée called time on the Italian stage of his career and returned to France to join Strasbourg.

Franck was with Strasbourg for two seasons. He notched nine goals in fifty-seven games and once again reached the final of the French Cup. This time, though, his quest for a Coupe de France winner's medal was not successful. In 1996, Sauzée moved on to Montpellier. Things started well there but in his final season, a young coach, Jean-Louis Gasset, perceived Franck as a threat and broke off communication with him. In February 1999, after he had made forty-six appearances for them, scoring nine goals in the process, Montpellier allowed Franck Sauzée to join Hibs.

Hibs fans could hardly believe that their club had acquired a man who had won the UEFA Champion's League, collected four French league winner's medals, two French Cup winner's medals and two runners-up medals in the same competition, played in well over 400 club matches and scored more than 100 career goals. He had captained his country and played for France thirty-nine times with great success, building up an impressive goal-scoring record in the process.

It may have seemed too good to be true but it wasn't. Alex McLeish's signing of Franck Sauzée was to prove inspired. Sauzée was to embrace Hibernian and all it stood for and, in so doing, create a legacy of commitment and class that continues to burn strongly.

Back in the depths of the 1998–99 winter, though, the great man's challenge was to help his new club complete the task of securing promotion to the SPL. By the time Franck Sauzée arrived at Easter Road, Hibs were on track for a swift return to the top flight. It is fair to say, however, that the club's promotion campaign had not got off to the most promising of starts.

2

THE PUSH FOR PROMOTION

WHEN FRANCK SAUZÉE and his new Hibernian colleagues finally left the rain-soaked Brockville pitch after his debut match and headed for the warmth of the dressing rooms, they could reflect on a job extremely well done. The match they had just won had been the proverbial 'six-pointer'. Hibs had travelled to Falkirk with a healthy but not yet decisive lead in the First Division title race. Defeat would have thrown the fight for promotion wide open again. The hard fought victory they had secured through a combination of grit and quality football had opened a gap between them and their nearest challenger, which could only be closed by a succession of defeats for Hibs and a run of wins for Falkirk. If promotion wasn't quite signed and sealed just yet, there was no doubt that a significant step towards confirming a return to the Scottish Premier League had been taken.

Hibs were now in a good place but no one would have applied that description to where they had found themselves at the start of season 1998–99. It was both embarrassing and financially damaging for a club of Hibs stature to find itself in the First Division. They would lose television income and gate revenue and the prospect of failing to secure promotion at the first time of asking didn't bear thinking about.

As the season got underway, Hibs fans had a lot to reflect on. Four directors had left the club and two new ones had come in. The new men were Malcolm McPherson and Steven Dunn. They were on the board to apply their business expertise and neither had to justify being there. Their credentials as committed supporters of Hibernian FC were impeccable.

Half of Easter Road had now been redeveloped and there were splendid new stands at the North and South ends of the ground. At a pre-season friendly match against Barnsley, the North Stand was renamed the Famous Five Stand and the four surviving members of that great Hibs forward line were there to grace the occasion. The late Willie Ormond's widow completed the quintet.

Gordon Smith, in fact, moved with such grace when he was introduced to the crowd that some supporters had wondered if it was worth signing him as a player for the season ahead! The fact that Gordon was now in his seventies made that possibility rather unlikely. There was no doubt, though, that seeing players from the team's glory days made the fans feel a little better as they realised that Hibs had enjoyed their great times and that the club could rise again.

Chairman Tom O'Malley, another lifelong Hibee, built on this early feel-good factor when he commented that Hibs had much to thank their marvellous fans for. He expressed the hope that the club's followers would stand by them in their hour of need. It is unlikely that either he or the supporters he praised realised at that point just how acute that hour of need was to become in the early part of the season.

There hadn't just been change in the boardroom over the close season. Players like Willie Miller, Stuart McCaffrey and Darren Dodds had chosen to move on rather than sample life in the First Division, but the biggest loss to the playing staff was that of Grant Brebner.

When Alex McLeish had first joined Hibs with twelve games of season 1997–98 left to play, he had gone to his old boss Alex Ferguson (he wasn't a knight of the realm at that time) and asked the great man if he had someone who could do a job for Hibs on loan. Fergie had provided the aforesaid Brebner and the midfielder had made an instant impression.

Cultured on the ball and a neat passer with an eye for goal, Brebner, who came from Midlothian, was also a Hibs supporter. He very quickly endeared himself to the fans and when Hibs were eventually relegated after a defeat at home to Dundee United, no one had done more on the pitch to try to avoid that fate than the lad from Old Trafford.

At the end of the season, Alex Ferguson made it clear that if Brebner wanted to make his move to Hibs permanent, he would not stand in his way, as long as he received a fee for the player that he considered reflected his worth. This gave Hibs supporters a much-needed boost but their euphoria didn't last very long as Brebner, like many a modern footballer before and since, put financial gain before love of a club and signed for Reading instead.

Alex McLeish, meanwhile, realised the major challenge that lay ahead of him. He was also aware, though, that he had the backing of a magnificent support. McLeish had done his best to keep Hibs up and had very nearly succeeded. In the end, the task had proved just too much for him. One of the last games of the season had been at Dunfermline. The Hibs squad had eaten lunch in Fife and, as they ate, they looked out of the hotel window to see hordes of their club's fans passing by en route to East End Park. The manager had instructed his players to leave the table and go outside to mingle with their supporters so that they might appreciate just how special the Hibs support was.

McLeish wanted the very best for that support and he hatched an ambitious plan to sign the great Peter Beardsley. What a coup that would have been. Unfortunately, the move didn't materialise, so the manager turned his attention elsewhere. He signed Stuart Lovell from Reading. Lovell wasn't well known in Scotland but his scoring record of sixty-seven goals in 150 appearances for his previous club was more than respectable. Another McLeish capture was Paul Holsgrove. Holsgrove was a midfielder who had plied his trade in the lower English leagues. Most Hibs fans would rather have had Grant Brebner, although they were fully aware that the club had done everything possible to make that particular deal happen.

A large travelling support followed Hibs to Cappielow for the first game in their new league. Their hosts, Morton, were more than up for the challenge but a tremendous late goal from Barry Lavety secured the three points.

So far, so good but disaster was just around the corner. Hibs' opening home match in the First Division was against Stranraer and amazingly almost 10,000 of their faithful supporters turned up to cheer them on. Stranraer were perennial strugglers and usually had the epithet 'lowly' appended to their name in newspaper reports. Everyone expected a comfortable home victory and everyone got the shock of their lives.

Hibs pounded the visitors' defense but had only a Tony Rougier goal to show for their efforts. Stranraer had two shots in the whole game – a penalty kick needlessly conceded by Holsgrove and a twenty-yard wonder strike from Jason Young, son of the former Hearts and Everton great, Alex. Both flew into the Hibs net and gave the team, from the town best known as the base from which ferries leave for Ireland, a famous win.

This was calamitous. Alex McLeish, in the programme for the next home match, remarked, 'Not for a minute did I think that I would be writing these notes after a home defeat from Stranraer.' Every Hibs supporter shared the manager's shock.

Things were to get worse before they got better. Six games into the league campaign, Hibs sat sixth in the ten-team First Division, having managed only two victories. The loss to Stranraer had been followed by another at Paisley against St Mirren. Even more worryingly, games against Hamilton at home and Clydebank away had been disappointingly drawn. To compound these early season woes, an encouraging League Cup win over Aberdeen had been followed by a four-goal capitulation to St Johnstone in Perth in the next round. Five thousand Hibs fans had travelled through to that game and salt had been rubbed into their wounds by a commanding midfield performance from former player and fanatical supporter

Paul Kane, who was now playing his football at McDiarmid Park. Further irony came in the shape of St Johnstone's fourth goal being scored by John O'Neil. O'Neil was to join Hibs less than two years later.

Hibs' manager remained bullish in public, though. He declared, 'I believe we have the players who can do a whole lot better than current form suggests.' Behind the scenes, things were a little different. McLeish knew his squad needed strengthening.

He went to Chief Executive Rod Petrie and told him frankly, 'Rod, I can't guarantee that I can take you up with this group of players. I need to add players who can make a difference, players I call "game breakers".'

To his credit, Petrie pledged the support of himself and the club's board. McLeish made excellent use of this backing to produce three inspired signings before the end of the season. Prior to these players being signed, the manager was working with the nucleus of the side that had taken the club down.

In goal, Oli Gottskalksson, for whom Jim Duffy had paid far too much a season earlier, had been restored. When Alex McLeish had originally taken over at Easter Road, he had signed Bryan Gunn from Norwich to replace the big Icelander. Gunn had done well but was now out injured after breaking his leg in pre-season training. Sadly, the big man from Thurso was never able to recover fully from this blow and, later in the season, was forced to call time on his career.

John Hughes and Shaun Dennis brought experience and physical presence, if not pace, to central defence, while Pat McGinlay, now thirty-one years old, continued to work hard and pose a goal threat in midfield. McGinlay was supported by Justin Skinner, who had been signed from Bristol Rovers by McLeish not long after his arrival as manager. Skinner was a cultured player who brought composure on the ball and passing ability to the centre of the park. Just before he came to Hibs, Skinner had been invited to play a trial for Stoke. The day before the trial match was due to take place, the Potters then manager, Chris Kamara, was sacked. His counterpart at Easter Road wasted no time in moving in and signing the midfielder. Hibs had benefited from Kamara's dismissal but it turned out to be a blessing in disguise for the man himself, too, as he landed a job with Sky Sports and is still one of the station's most popular pundits.

Up front, Stevie Crawford was mobile and skilful but capable of scoring more frequently than he had in Hibs' relegation season. His partner was Barry Lavety. Bulky of build but possessed of surprising skill for a big man, 'Basher' scored some superb goals. However, as his record of forty-eight goals in five seasons with St Mirren before joining Hibs showed, he was never likely to be prolific. Crawford and Lavety were joined in the front line by Tony Rougier.

Rougier could beat defenders for fun and had all the talent in the world, but he had to be in the mood first. With his languid temperament and reluctance to break sweat, Tony's form was best described as intermittent. The Trinidadian's attitude was summed up by his experience of the game of cricket. Recalling that he had been a very good cricketer, he added that running in to bowl fast hadn't been for him, so he had concentrated on batting instead. Although quite good with a bat in his hand, Tony hadn't relished being hit by a hard ball coming down at him at a rate of knots. He had therefore given up cricket altogether and taken up football!

McLeish had originally added to his basic squad by signing the aforementioned Holsgrove and Lovell. He now moved onto the market again and signed two Austrians, an Irishman and a Finn. The Austrians were Klaus Dietrich and Peter Guggi and they didn't last long.

One look at central defender Dietrich in a Hibs jersey was enough for McLeish and Guggi only managed a few more appearances. He actually looked a decent midfield player and scored a couple of excellent goals. However, he managed to get himself into the tabloid newspapers for non-footballing reasons not long after arriving in Edinburgh and he too was soon on his way.

Barry Prenderville, an Irish right back, came on loan from Coventry and settled in immediately. Apart from his sound defensive play, he demonstrated an ability to overlap and a shot that would bring him goals.

The Finn was Mixu Paatelainen. Big Mixu had impressed in Scotland with both Aberdeen and Dundee United before moving South. He had gone to Bolton where he initially did well, even playing in a League Cup Final at Wembley. Mixu had then moved on to Wolverhampton Wanderers, where he had been less successful. During season 1997–98, he had made twenty-three appearances for Mark McGhee's side but had failed to score a single goal.

For a man whose previous career record had been seventy-one goals in 277 games, this was very disappointing. There had always been more to Paatelainen's game than goal scoring. He held the ball up superbly and was expert at bringing other players into the game, but he was now approaching his thirty-second birthday and his recent form suggested that his best days might be behind him. When Hibs fans heard that Alex McLeish had spent £75,000 on a striker who hadn't scored a single goal in the previous season, they thought that their manager had paid far too much. They couldn't have been more wrong. Paatelainen turned out to be a revelation and an inspired signing.

While Hibs' manager retained confidence in his players – he had even felt able to sell the speedy, skilful but inconsistent Kevin Harper to Derby County – his confidence was not shared by the club's supporters. Indeed, the discontent in the stands was pronounced enough for chairman Tom O'Malley to record in the match programme at the end of September that 'continuing unrest off the field is affecting the atmosphere in the stadium, making it difficult for the manager and players'.

Things began to improve while the personnel continued to change. Derek Anderson, yet another central defender, came in from Kilmarnock. Anderson's career at Easter Road was to last a mere six games as Alex McLeish relentlessly shuffled his pack. A young striker called Kenny Miller had shown some early season promise. He was sent out on loan to Stenhousemuir to gain experience.

An impressive 3–1 win away to Airdrie, a team who had caused Hibs many problems over the years, was a sign of better things to come. This match was notable, too, for Paatelainen scoring his first Hibs goal. Then came a transfer of major importance. Hibs eighth signing of season 1998–99 was a certain Russell Latapy.

Hibs travelled to Ayr on 24 October on the back of wins in their last two games. Late goals from Lovell and McGinlay had ensured victories at Stranraer and against Morton at home and Hibs were now top of the league, two points ahead of Falkirk. Their hosts at Somerset Park were also very much involved in the fight for promotion.

Hibs' improved form looked short-lived as they trailed Ayr 3–1 with only a few minutes remaining. However, goals from captain John Hughes (his second of the game) and Paatelainen showed the team's fighting spirit and earned a draw that felt like a victory. Latapy had made his debut in this match and had been impressive. His performance had moved his manager to state: 'Russell is a very comfortable and competent player. He looks good on the ball, passes well and has confidence.'

Latapy now began to make his presence felt. He inspired wins over Raith Rovers and Clydebank but managed to get sent off against Hamilton at Firhill. The Accies were playing their home games at Partick's stadium because they had sold their own ground at Douglas Park. Most people felt that Russell's dismissal was harsh and his ten remaining colleagues contrived to surrender a two goal lead in the last fifteen minutes and throw away two points.

One newspaper report spoke of Latapy dominating midfield in the same way as his cricketing friend Brian Lara dominated bowling attacks. He had certainly added something extra to Hibs' play and the team now began to perform much better and really get into its stride as it pushed for promotion.

Stuart Lovell, who had been fairly quiet since signing, scored two fine goals in a 4–1 demolition of St Mirren at home and he was on target again as Airdrie and Morton were defeated. Hibs' third goal at Cappielow was scored by Tony Rougier and it was to prove his last for the club, as not long afterwards he was sold to Port Vale.

The dressing room door at Easter Road must have been dizzy as it was constantly opened and closed by players leaving and arriving. Hibs faced a crucial match against their main title challengers Falkirk on Saturday, 12 December. The importance of this match is shown in the attendance. For the first time in the season, over 10,000 supporters turned out for a match at Easter Road. Goals by Hughes and Crawford sealed a 2–1 win and sent the fans home happy.

There were two more new faces in the Hibs ranks as McLeish continued to strengthen his squad. Clydebank left back Paul Lovering, all energy and enthusiasm, had caught the eye playing against Hibs and was duly acquired. Coventry had refused to let Barry Prenderville extend his loan spell, which was a pity because he had become popular with the Hibs crowd and had even managed two goals in his thirteen appearances. Undaunted, McLeish then signed Morton right back Derek Collins. Collins was a calm, assured player who was unlikely to rival Prenderville in the goal-scoring stakes. His most famous counter had been a twenty-five-yard rocket against Rangers in a 3–2 Morton win ten years earlier, but with just eleven goals in over 400 appearances at Cappielow, he could hardly be described as a prolific scorer. Mind you, he was to score a very significant goal before the season was out.

The win over Falkirk was followed by a 3–0 victory over Clydebank at Easter Road on the last Saturday before Christmas, which allowed Hibs to open up a six-point lead at the top of the league. Russell Latapy got his first Hibs goal in this game and he was already a firm favourite with the Hibs support. The admiration was mutual as the little Trinidadian declared, 'The Hibs fans are great. They accepted me at once and there is a really special feeling about this club.'

That special feeling led to gates of over 14,000 for the matches against Ayr and Raith Rovers on Boxing Day and 2 January. Hibs won both, scoring eight goals in the process and the feel-good factor had really returned to Easter Road.

The board continued to provide magnificent backing for its manager and yet another new arrival was the twenty-two-year-old Raith Rovers right winger Paul Hartley who, having been acquired with the money raised by the sale of Tony Rougier, made his debut against Ayr. At one point in the game, Hartley, stationed on the right touch line kicking up the slope (which still existed in early 1999), controlled a waist-high cross-field pass with exquisite touch and set off towards the Ayr goal, keeping the ball in the air as he went. One fan shouted, 'I've never seen anyone do that since Gordon Smith was here.' This comparison was to prove a shade premature, although Hartley was to play his part in Hibs' promotion surge. His career didn't really fully take off until he joined Hearts from St Johnstone after leaving Easter Road. At this early point in his time as a Hibs player, however, he looked very promising indeed.

The crowd against Raith Rovers on 2 January was just under 15,000 and the second largest in the whole of Scotland. The Hibs fans were happy to see their team on course for a return to Scottish football's top flight. Another home game against Hamilton followed. Again the crowd exceeded the 10,000 mark and the Accies, always difficult opponents, were summarily dispatched by four goals to nil.

Pat McGinlay, recalling his great days as a goal-scoring midfielder in his first spell as a Hibs player, now had twelve goals for the season. Big Mixu, who hadn't managed a solitary goal the previous season, had eleven and Stevie Crawford wasn't far behind on eight. New signing Derek Collins professed himself amazed at the 'sheer size of Hibernian'.

It seemed like nothing could stop the Hibees now, although St Mirren did try. When Hibs visited Paisley, the referee did his best to assist the Buddies by harshly sending off Stevie Crawford for an alleged dive. It was the striker's twenty-fifth birthday and the card that the referee produced was not the kind that Stevie was looking for.

Hibs, undeterred with yet another new signing in Tom Smith from Clydebank in their ranks, went on to win 2–1 with another goal from Paatelainen and a strike from Hartley, his first for the club. Hibs fans were starting to realise what it must be like to support the Old Firm. Their gates were far bigger than those of their rivals, their travelling support regularly outnumbered home fans at away games and if somebody played well against them, they could strengthen their own team while simultaneously weakening their rivals by signing these players. Paul Lovering, Derek Collins and Tom Smith were all examples of the benefits of cherrypicking.

Soon it was Scottish Cup time. Hibs had won twelve league matches in a row and couldn't have asked for a better draw than lower division Stirling Albion at home. No Hibs fan reading this book will be surprised to learn that Albion knocked the greens out of the cup after a replay. If league form was at an all-time high, then Hibs' cup performances had plumbed the depths. Injured team captain John Hughes, ordinarily positivity personified, proved himself to be a master of understatement when he admitted, 'The cups just haven't worked out for us this season.'

Usually, a Scottish Cup defeat spreads gloom amongst the Hibernian faithful but this season was different. There was only one priority and that was promotion. When the league programme resumed, Stranraer were defeated 2–0 at Easter Road. What came next was the visit to Brockville.

3

THE ARRIVAL OF MONSIEUR SAUZÉE

THIS MATCH was seminal. A Falkirk win would have thrown the race for the First Division title wide open again. Falkirk didn't win of course and not even the most cautious of Hibs supporters (and the author of this book is a fully paid up member of that particular club) could still have doubts about their team's imminent return to the top flight.

Not only had Derek Collins, the full back who scored only infrequently, notched the vital winning goal, but the great Franck Sauzée had also made his Hibernian bow in the Falkirk wind and rain. When Sauzée ran out in the famous green and white for the first time, most Hibs fans' minds would have gone back to George Best's debut at Paisley twenty years earlier. They were pinching themselves and asking, 'Is Franck Sauzée really a Hibs player?'

Well, he undoubtedly was and Hibs now had two high-class players in their ranks in Sauzée and Latapy. When Hibs next travelled to Ayr, the two great men showed early signs of the telepathic combination that was to prove so beguiling in the seasons ahead. The 'Honest Men' were beaten 3–1 and Stevie Crawford took centre stage with a fine hat trick. The more discerning supporters inside Somerset Park that day, though, saw most hope for the future in the undoubted quality of Sauzée and Latapy.

This league win was Hibs' thirteenth in a row but complacency brought this impressive record to an end when, in front of 1,695 spectators at Boghead, Clydebank turned the formbook on its head to win 2–0. Franck Sauzée, who had played in front of huge crowds in the world's greatest stadiums, must have wondered what he had let himself in for on that dismal day.

Franck and Hibs fans needn't have worried. Hibs learned from this lapse and very quickly got back to winning ways. When Sauzée made his long awaited home debut against Airdrie on Saturday, 20 March, it was, due to a quirk of the fixtures computer, Hibs' first home match for six weeks.

Alex McLeish, in his programme notes, sounded most statesmanlike as he proclaimed, 'Since I last spoke to you, I have signed two French players.' He added, 'They will be looking forward to playing in front of the home fans (if selected!).' One has to assume that the manager's tongue was firmly in his cheek, as he must surely have been hardly able to believe his luck that such a great player as Sauzée had chosen to commit himself to Hibs.

McLeish had been determined to make a marquee signing. He had his sights on Phillipe Albert, the classy Belgian centre back at Newcastle United and Emil Kostadinov, the highly rated Bulgarian striker was also on his radar. When he heard that Sauzée was available, however, there was only one target. Now, like the Canadian Mounted Police, he had got his man.

The Hibs manager had long been a student of football all over the globe. He subscribed to *World Soccer* magazine and had a vast knowledge of who was playing where and what sort of form they were in. Such was his meticulousness that Stuart Lovell remembers him questioning referees after games: 'He would ask them whether they knew about refereeing in Europe. If they had, he would ask them specifically about foreign match officials and their approach to the game.

'It was his intention to find out as much as he could regarding a particular individual's style of refereeing, such as whether they were particularly strict on high-footed tackles or dissent or indeed if they were lenient in other areas. I never played for any other manager who did this,' recalls Lovell.

Looking back now, Big Alex recalls, 'The Bosman ruling opened doors for clubs like Hibs. It meant that we could sign top players without paying a transfer fee as long as we were willing to pay decent wages. When I told Franck about the way Hibs supporters liked their team to play and the great Hibs teams of the fifties and seventies, he didn't need much persuading to join up at Easter Road. However, the Bosman ruling also had a detrimental effect from the point of view that it hampered the progress of young players. Hibs went in a different direction a couple of years later with the emergence of some great youngsters.'

Sauzée wasn't difficult to deal with financially either. Former chairman Malcolm McPherson remembers, 'Franck made only one demand. That was that no one at the club should be paid more than him. He didn't mind someone being paid the same as he was. He just would not accept anyone being paid more.'

The other French player McLeish had signed, incidentally, was Alex Marinkov. Marinkov, a raw-boned centre half, had done the rounds of the French lower leagues before coming to England to sign for Scarborough. Almost all of his teams in his home country had won promotion while he played for them and he was keen to continue this run of success as he joined his more illustrious compatriot at Easter Road.

In taking Marinkov from Yorkshire, McLeish finally completed his season's work in the transfer market (there were no set signing windows in the late nineties). He had brought in nine players, three of whom he had allowed to leave again after a short period.

This spoke volumes for the manager's determination to keep strengthening his team. It was also a testament to the club's board's willingness to support McLeish in his quest to not only win the First Division but also to lay the foundations for a successful return to the SPL.

There is no doubt that Alex McLeish had the SPL in mind when he signed Franck Sauzée. The three months or so Hibs had left in the First Division would allow Sauzée to find his feet in Scotland.

By the time the new season came round, he would be fully integrated at Easter Road and ready for the bigger challenge of the top league. Sauzée revealed, not long after signing, that he had been given the opportunity to talk to FC Basle, Toulouse and Rapid Vienna, but the prospect of coming to Edinburgh had appealed to him most. This, and Alex McLeish's persuasiveness and prestige, were what enabled Hibs to secure what one newspaper called 'the biggest ever name in the Scottish First Division'.

Sauzée had not only impressed Alex McLeish and Andy Watson with his footballing skills during his original few days in Scotland – they knew how good a player he was already – he had also shown them that he retained a hunger for success and that his general fitness, if not his match fitness, was excellent. According to McLeish, Sauzée had 'flown through' his medical.

On Sauzée's first day of training with Hibs during his initial visit, he had played things in a low-key manner, introducing himself to his prospective new team mates simply by his first name. Centre half Shaun Dennis admitted after Sauzée had signed up at Easter Road, 'We knew the face but couldn't quite place this big guy who was introduced to us as "Frank". It didn't take us long, though, to realise that he was in fact the great Franck Sauzée.' Nobody in Scotland would fail to recognise Franck Sauzée again. That was for sure.

When Hibs successfully disposed of their old nemesis Airdrie 3–0 at Easter Road, Franck Sauzée got a taste of the more combative side of Scottish football when he was lucky to escape injury after being caught by a late tackle from Steve Cooper. Young Kenny Miller had also now returned from a prolific loan spell at Stenhousemuir, so another piece of the jigsaw was in place.

Hibs' next fixture took them to Firhill to face homeless but always obdurate Hamilton Academicals. On the same day, 3 April 1999, Falkirk would play Morton. If Hibs won and Falkirk lost, nothing could stop the First Division title being claimed by Hibs.

Hibs did indeed win and did so in style. Spurred on by a large travelling support, they were way too good for Accies and as well as cheering their own team's triumph, the Hibs fans were able to rejoice in Falkirk's demise at Cappielow, which ensured that the First Division Championship flag could now only fly at Easter Road.

Hibs won 2–0 with both goals coming from Russell Latapy. 'The little magician', as he was now widely known, stole the show. Time and again, he ran at the Hamilton defence, twisting and turning and causing all sorts of problems. Twice, Russell linked superbly with Mixu Paatelainen and went on to shoot powerfully past Ian McFarlane in the Hamilton goal.

Latapy's display drew lavish praise from both the press and his team mates. One national newspaper described his play as 'pure magic' and compared him with SPL stars like Paul Gascoigne, Brian Laudrup, Paolo Di Canio and Henrik Larsson.

His Trinidad and Tobago colleague Dwight Yorke, who at that point was at the peak of his career and on the verge of winning a historic treble of League, FA Cup and Champions League with Manchester United, simply said, 'Russell is the most talented player I have ever played alongside.' That was quite a compliment.

After defeating Hamilton, the Hibs players ran a lap of honour. Their supporters acclaimed their achievement and treasured their performance. Some of them even invaded the pitch to congratulate their heroes and celebrate with them. Latapy may have taken most of the plaudits but the game, like the whole season, had not been a one-man show. Everyone had contributed.

Paatelainen, in his usual understated and probably underrated manner, led the line superbly. Big Shaun Dennis at the back was an impassable barrier and then there was Franck Sauzée. Franck was now wearing the number four shirt and partnering Latapy in central midfield. He was playing just in front of the back four and providing his gifted colleague with the freedom to play higher up the field and fully commit himself to attack. This is what Alex McLeish had envisaged happening when he had signed Sauzée and his plan had really begun to come to fruition that day at Firhill.

Demonstrably fitter now, Sauzée was making and winning tackles in majestic fashion. He was also using the ball superbly. At the start of the season, Hibs had given the ball away regularly. Now, mindful of Jock Stein's oft repeated dictum of 'If we've got the ball, then the other team can't score', the team was retaining possession impressively. There were two reasons for this. One was called Franck Sauzée and the other was called Russell Latapy.

Latapy should really have had a hat trick against Hamilton, as he missed a second half penalty. He was annoyed with himself, as his record from the spot was excellent and he hadn't missed too often from twelve yards during his career. It didn't really matter though. What was important was that Hibs were back where they belonged in the highest echelon of Scottish football.

Shaun Dennis summed up what many Hibs supporters were thinking when he said, 'This means everything to the players and the fans, who have been magnificent throughout.' He added, 'We are a better team now and much more equipped to perform in the Premier League than we have been in the past.'

Chairman Tom O'Malley told it as it was when he said, 'After a nervous start, the Championship was won by the length of Leith Walk.' O'Malley, his fellow directors and then Managing Director, Rod Petrie, deserved great credit for the manner in which they had backed Alex McLeish.

The manager himself stressed the need for continued application in the five league games that remained. He did not want to see his team drop its guard or lower its standards. He needn't have worried. Hibs were champions now, albeit at a lower level than they would have liked, and like all champions, they had pride in their performance and a desire to keep winning.

The win at Hamilton had been followed by a trip to Stark's Park, Kirkcaldy and another convincing away victory against Raith Rovers. Shaun Dennis scored against his old team and Latapy was on target once more. Sauzée for his part was now starting to really make his mark. In this match he 'showed the touches and presence which made him such a great success in France'. He also had some words of wisdom for the Hibs support.

Recalling his time at Sochaux and how that team had won every single league match in the process of achieving promotion, Franck stressed that this success had provided a platform for the club to go on and win the French Cup and compete in Europe. He hoped that Hibs could do something similar.

He made the point that he had been happy to leave Montpellier because his relationship with Jean-Louis Gasset, his coach there, had completely broken down. He couldn't see that happening with Alex McLeish. He revealed that they had clicked from the word go and that he had been 'honoured and embarrassed' by McLeish's deep knowledge of his international career for France.

Franck also said that former Hearts goalkeeper Gilles Rousset, an old international colleague and friend of his, had told him to go to Hibs. He had already realised that Rousset had given him very good advice indeed.

It was becoming clear that Alex McLeish had pulled off a once in a generation coup in signing Franck Sauzée. This hugely talented footballer was not only pleasingly modest, he had clearly decided that Easter Road was not a stopping off place for him, but somewhere where he would be happy and at home and where he would endeavour to play his very best football. This man, only the fifth Hibernian player to win a European Cup winner's medal (Bertie Auld, George Best, Des Bremner and Ronnie Simpson were the others), had fully embraced the Hibs way of life. It was already evident that Franck loved Hibs. The Hibs support, man, woman and child, loved him in return.

The signing of Latapy had also been an inspired move and he and his new midfield partner were really starting to dovetail. Describing the win at Raith, one reporter got it absolutely right when he wrote, 'Franck Sauzée in the Hibernian midfield had an excellent game and much of what was good by Hibs came from his cultured feet.' Nor was the same scribe wrong when he added, 'Russell Latapy was again in fine form and he opened the scoring with a super solo run which left the Raith defenders befuddled and bewildered.'

When St Mirren next visited Easter Road, Franck came close to scoring his first goal when he headed against the upright. The man who got the first goal in the hard fought 2–1 win, though, was Paul Hartley. Hartley's stunning eighteen-yard shot flew into the roof of the net, leading to the prediction that he was 'on course to have a glittering career in green'. However, this forecast was not to prove one hundred per cent accurate.

Latapy continued his outstanding form by scoring the winning goal five minutes from time. St Mirren had been resolute in defence but their resistance was broken when the little maestro 'used his sublime skills to open what had appeared to be a locked door and notch the match winner with commendable composure'.

Hibs supporters were just beginning to fully realise that their team now contained two supreme players and that the club might be on the verge of something very exciting in the seasons ahead. Latapy, after all, was a man who had twice won the Portuguese League with Porto, in 1995 and 1996, and the Portuguese Cup with Boavista in 1997. He was a player of top pedigree and yet, thanks to a casual remark from the departing Tony Rougier, he had found his way to Easter Road via a trial match on a cold night in Brechin. It was quite amazing really, as was the capture of Sauzée. As mentioned, the French legend was now much fitter than he had been when he first arrived and this enhanced fitness was evident in his play.

Morton were next to visit Easter Road and Sauzée, in his eighth Hibs appearance, got on the score sheet for the first time. Initially, it had looked as if he was once again going to be denied when he crashed a free kick against the junction of the post and bar. Morton in fact took the lead through Derek Anderson, who had been signed then released by Alex McLeish earlier in the season, but Stuart Lovell, now playing in midfield and scoring regularly, soon levelled the scores.

Then came Franck's moment. A Russell Latapy corner reached him thirty yards from goal. He struck the ball beautifully on the volley and it flew low into the Morton net past goalkeeper Ally Maxwell. Such was the velocity and ferocity of Sauzée's strike that the ball had entered the net before the former Motherwell and Rangers man had time to even contemplate reacting.

Bedlam followed. The crowd erupted and Franck himself ran off in wild celebration. As his team mates attempted to catch up with Sauzée to congratulate him, the Frenchman removed his shirt and swung it above his head in triumph as he continued his turbo charged celebratory run. This act of spontaneous joy cost Franck a booking, of course, but neither he nor the Hibs fans in the ground were at all bothered by that. It had been a landmark Hibee moment and it would be a memory to treasure.

Sauzée's strike won the game for Hibs and he revealed afterwards why, with over a hundred career goals already to his name, he had celebrated it with such gusto. Franck explained that, as it was his first ever Hibs goal, it was special and he wanted the supporters to know just how much it meant to him.

Franck sat out Hibs' next match, which was the penultimate game of the season away to Stranraer. Kenny Miller got his first ever goal for the club and Lovell, Crawford and Hartley were all on target as Hibs strolled to an easy 4–0 victory despite the manager making a number of changes to rest some of his main players. This canter in the Galloway sunshine seemed a long, long way removed from that cataclysmic and inexplicable early season defeat to the same opposition at Easter Road the previous August.

The stage was now set for the season's finale. Falkirk would visit Easter Road for this final encounter of the 1998–99 campaign. They were second in the league but were now a distant twenty points behind Hibs. A full house was expected and the First Division Trophy would be presented at the end of the match. Alex McLeish made it very clear to his players in the days leading up to the game that he wanted this special occasion for players and fans alike to be exactly that. He wanted no slip-ups and no anti-climax. Falkirk, for their part, with experienced and proud professionals like Scott Crabbe, Marino Keith, Kevin McAllister and Ivo den Bieman in their ranks, would be doing everything they could to spoil the party.

As the Hibs squad drove to the ground, the atmosphere on the team coach was light hearted. McLeish made a pretence of fining Franck Sauzée for using his mobile phone. The player responded by handing his manager a ten-pound note. Once in the dressing room, though, the mood changed. The manager reminded his players of the additional training they had done in the lead up to the match to gain what he called that 'extra edge'. He finished by exhorting the team to go out and show themselves to be worthy champions.

Hibs took the field to be greeted by a near capacity crowd. They didn't get off to the best of starts, though. Shaun Dennis rose to head a ball clear and referee Alan Freeland, no stranger to controversy, awarded the softest of penalty kicks for what he presumably adjudged to be 'leaning on' by the centre half. Former Hearts man Crabbe strode forward. He hit a powerful shot to the goalkeeper's right. The ball was at a saveable height, though, and Oli Gottskalksson, an ever-present all season, dived to make a fine save. The crowd, already in boisterous mood, now became positively rowdy.

Soon, Hibs were ahead. They were awarded a free kick in a central area around thirty yards from goal. Sauzée and Latapy stood over the ball. The little Trinidadian rolled the ball a couple of yards forward and Sauzée came on to it and struck it with immense force. His shot seemed to gather pace as it flew through the air and it thundered past the Falkirk goalkeeper Myles Hogarth into the top left-hand corner of the net. The strike was like a ballistic missile and the Hibs support went ballistic, too. After receiving the congratulations of his team mates, big Franck ran across to the dugout and hugged his manager. There was clearly the strongest of bonds between the two men.

Early in the second half, Mixu Paatelainen and Stevie Crawford linked up as they had been doing all season. Hogarth blocked Crawford's shot but Paul Hartley appeared from nowhere to head the rebound into the net. The game was now effectively over and it was simply a case of waiting for the celebrations to begin.

When the post-match celebrations did take place, they were well worth waiting for. Captain John Hughes, recently returned from injury, lifted the First Division Trophy on high, Alex McLeish –who had been the subject of speculation that he might be leaving Hibs to return to Aberdeen – assured the fans that he was going nowhere and Franck Sauzée yelled, 'Vive Les Hibs, Vive L'Écosse, Vive La France.' Back in the dressing room, no one celebrated more enthusiastically than Sauzée. When he wasn't spraying champagne, he was drinking it.

Ian Murray, who has served Hibs so well over the best part of ten years, was an eighteen-year-old youngster at Easter Road at the time of the promotion campaign. After the Falkirk match, he approached Franck Sauzée and asked if he could have his First Division Championship t-shirt. With typical generosity, Franck agreed and signed the top before handing it over to the young player. Ian has that memento to this day.

Hibs had finished the season a full twenty-three points in front of second place Falkirk. Having taken just fifteen points from a possible twenty-seven in the first quarter of the season, Hibs had followed up with twenty-three, the maximum twenty-seven and twenty-four from the final three quarters of the campaign.

Indeed, in their final twenty-seven matches, they had gained seventy-four points out of a possible eighty-one on offer. This was championship-winning form indeed. Just how far Alex McLeish had cast his net in search of quality was shown by the fact that he had used no fewer than thirty-two players in the course of the season. Four of these players, Crawford, Lovell, McGinlay and Paatelainen had achieved double figures in terms of the number of goals they had scored.

Promotion had been well and truly secured and McLeish summed the season up succinctly when he said, 'In the first quarter of the season, we realised the size of our task. From the second quarter on, helped by our great support, we began to win regularly.

By the end of the season, we weren't just winning, we were winning with style.'

The style referred to had been in supplied in no little measure by two players – Russell Latapy and Franck Sauzée. This duo would be the key to Hibs making a successful return to the Scottish Premier League.

The good news for Hibs fans was that both men were well up for the challenge. Latapy was thirty and Sauzée thirty-three but both had been re-energised by their moves to Easter Road. Their happiness with their place of work was reflected in their play.

While admitting that Sauzée no longer possessed the pace of his halcyon days, Alex McLeish was quick to add that Franck was 'five yards quicker upstairs than any other player'. He also added that the French playmaker had transformed Hibs' play through his composure and passing ability. He had also allowed Latapy to take up a more advanced role and that too had proved significant.

Latapy himself couldn't have been happier. He revealed that he had such good feelings about Hibs that he had bought books about the club's past. This had made him realise just how big a club he had come to. He was delighted that Hibs fans had taken to him immediately (he was a classic Hibs type of player, of course). His popularity had made him happy and helped him to play better.

So taken was little Russell with Hibs that he had thought to himself as he had played his trial match at Brechin, 'This may not be the Champions League which I am used to but I would like to be a part of this club.'

He was now an integral part of Hibernian FC alongside another outstanding footballer in Franck Sauzée. These two top players considered Hibs' prospects on their return to the Premier League to be very positive. Their optimism was shared by a Hibs support which only one year earlier had been in the depths of despair. For Hibs players and fans alike, season 1999–2000 could not come quickly enough.

4

SETTLING IN TO THE SPL

THE SPL WAS scheduled to make an early start in season 1999-2000. Hibs' first match would be against Motherwell at home and the game would take place on the last Saturday in July. The short summer break for Hibs supporters was pleasurable. They were able to bask in the glory of their First Division success, assess the team's new signings and anticipate the coming campaign with a measure of confidence.

The team that had ended the previous season was significantly stronger than that which had started it. The big question, though, was were Hibs good enough to hold their own or, even better, to flourish in the months ahead?

Alex McLeish, as was his wont, had been busy in the transfer market over the close season. He had signed four players.

Nick Colgan, an Irish under-21 international goalkeeper, had joined up from Bournemouth to fill the gap created by Bryan Gunn's retirement through injury. Colgan had spent seven years at Chelsea before his move to the South coast but had not been able to establish himself as a regular first choice at either of his previous clubs.

French midfielder Fabrice Henry was a former team mate of Franck Sauzée. Franck had recommended him, as had Hearts goalkeeper Gilles Rousset. One wondered why Rousset hadn't put a word in for Henry at his own club. Maybe he had and Jim Jefferies,

31

his manager, had felt well enough covered in the centre of the park. Henry came to Easter Road from Swiss club Basel and had turned down the chance to join Cagliari in the Italian League to do so.

Hibs' third new face was the German centre forward Dirk Lehmann. Lehmann came from Fulham where he had played under Kevin Keegan. If he could score as many goals for Hibs as his former manager had done for Liverpool and England, then no Hibs fan would be complaining.

McLeish's final summer recruit was also from Germany. Mathias Jack arrived from Fortuna Düsseldorf with a name as a rugged centre half with a bit of football in him. He also brought with him a reputation for volatility.

There was a change off the field, too. Having done a magnificent job in steering Hibs back to the top league, Tom O'Malley stepped aside from his responsibilities as chairman. Tom handed the baton to another lifelong Hibs supporter, the prominent Edinburgh lawyer Malcolm McPherson.

As the press and media indulged in their usual pre-season guessing games as to which Scottish club might be capable of challenging Celtic and Rangers in the coming term, they all raised doubts over the prospects of Hibs. The general consensus was that Hibs had relied very heavily on the talents of Franck Sauzée and Russell Latapy in their promotion push. Questions were asked about the ability of the new fans' favourites at Easter Road to replicate the success they had enjoyed to date in the SPL. After all, it was pointed out, Sauzée was approaching his thirty-fourth birthday and Latapy was also into his thirties.

Hibs' own supporters had no doubts whatsoever. They had seen enough of Franck and Russell to know that their club was in the fortunate position of having two very special players on its books.

Only nine weeks after celebrating winning the First Division and, after what Alex McLeish described as 'the shortest close season I can remember', Hibs were back in action. The club played four pre-season games in Denmark. They drew the first three but won the fourth, against amateur side Hornbaek, by every Hibee's favourite score of 7–0. Hornbaek is on the Danish coast and the local club was all at sea as Hibs piled up the goals. Justin Skinner contributed two from midfield and the highly promising Kenny Miller went one better with a fine hat trick.

There was an amusing but significant incident during one of the matches on this Danish tour. Franck Sauzée hit a magnificent fifty-yard pass to Russell Latapy. After the game, Franck apologised to Russell for his pass. 'Why are you apologising man?' said the little magician. 'It was a great pass.'

'It wasn't,' said Franck. 'You had to move a foot to your left to control it.' Sauzée was deadly serious and this comment spoke volumes about the standards he set for himself and for others.

There was one more friendly match before the serious stuff got under way. Hibs welcomed Bryan Robson's Middlesbrough to Easter Road. There was no shortage of big names in the Boro ranks. Australian Mark Schwarzer, who is still playing Premiership football thirteen years later, was in goal. Former Manchester United star Gary Pallister was the main man in central defence, while Andy Townsend and the one and only Paul Gascoigne were in central midfield.

Those who had questioned the ability of Sauzée and Latapy to make the transition from lower-league leading men to top rank players only needed to watch this match to have their answers. Franck and Russell completely dominated the midfield and put their Premiership opponents firmly in the shade. Latapy topped off his display with an excellent winning goal.

Now it was time for the real thing and over 13,000 fans crowded into Easter Road on a beautiful summer afternoon to welcome Hibs' first SPL visitors in over a year in the shape of Motherwell. Motherwell were managed by Billy Davies who was already exhibiting the qualities which would lead to managerial success down South.

The Fir Park squad contained some famous names. In goal was a man who had played over 100 games for Hibs. Andy Goram was now thirty-five years old and, it is fair to say, not as slim as he had been in his halcyon days. He was, however, still an outstanding goalkeeper.

Big Shaun Teale, who had performed so well for Aston Villa in a winning League Cup Final against Manchester United, was in central defence and on the wing was the former Chelsea and Everton maestro Pat Nevin. Nevin now talks extremely well on football for the BBC. In those days, he was still letting his feet do the talking.

Up front was a notable duo. Lee McCulloch – later, of course, of Rangers and Scotland – and John Spencer – like Nevin, a man who had strutted his stuff at Stamford Bridge – formed a real Little and Large striking partnership.

Two other members of the Well squad that day now have Hibs connections. Alex McLeish was to sign midfielder Derek Townsley two years later and Derek Adams was, of course, until recently Hibs assistant manager.

The strength of the Motherwell playing staff clearly reflected the level of investment that had been made by their chairman John Boyle, who at that time was spending freely in an attempt to return his club to its former glories.

In his programme notes, Alex McLeish stated that he was looking for his players to do themselves justice and send their fans home happy. In the event, although they didn't manage to win the game, Hibs succeeded in meeting both of their manager's aims.

There was a real carnival atmosphere in the ground as Hibs supporters revelled in being back in the big time. Their two big time players were in their element. Sauzée and Latapy took complete control of central midfield and provided a platform for their team to launch attack after attack. Only the excellence of Goram in the Motherwell goal stopped Hibs from building a commanding lead. Less streamlined than he had been at his peak (which had earned him the unflattering nickname of The Flying Pig in some quarters), The Goalie, to give him his more recognised soubriquet, showed that he was still one of the best in the business as he defied Hibs time and again.

Lehmann struck a fine shot to give Hibs a well-deserved lead but Pat Nevin, on as a substitute and, like Goram, now in the veteran stage of his career, displayed all his old skill and trickery and managed to head in an equalising goal. Undeterred, Hibs kept piling on the pressure and Lehmann restored their lead. This time, the tall German striker netted with a towering header.

Deep into stoppage time, another Motherwell substitute, Stevie Nicholas, snatched a goal that gave his team a share of the points that they hardly merited. When Stirling Albion had knocked Hibs out of the Scottish Cup in the previous season, Nicholas had been on target. His performance in the two cup matches against Hibs had prompted Motherwell to sign him. Now, he had popped up to hurt Hibs again.

Hibs fans went home happy with their team's performance if not the final result. Alex McLeish was in no doubt that his players had deserved a victory. He stated unequivocally, 'We were most unfortunate not to win this game.'

Lehmann had made an outstanding competitive debut and most people watching the game wondered why Fulham had let him go and why he hadn't scored more goals in his career to date. First appearances can be deceptive, though, which is why scouts make a habit of returning to watch a player on a number of occasions before making a final judgement. Lehmann was never really to reach the standards of his opening display in a Hibs jersey again.

Hibs' first away fixture on their return to the top flight was a trip to Dens Park to face Dundee, who, at that time, were financially sound and quite a force on their home ground. Sky Television had started to cover SPL matches on Sunday evenings. The games kicked off at the unusual time of 6.05pm and the satellite giant's cameras were in Dundee for Hibs' visit.

The viewers got a treat. Hibs fans had always been confident that Franck Sauzée and Russell Latapy would make the transition from the Scottish First Division to the Scottish Premier League with ease. Regular attenders at Easter Road knew that in the Frenchman and the Trinidadian, their club had captured a duo of diamonds. Their legs were not as young as they had once been but their football brains were still razor sharp and their sublime skills were undiminished by the years.

Anyone watching the Dens Park match that August Sunday night who had previously harboured doubts about the Hibs big two's ability to maintain their standards of the previous season, soon had these doubts well and truly dispelled.

Hibs again played with flair and freedom, with Franck and Russell at the heart of all their best play. However, the cavalier approach that McLeish's men adopted, while great to watch and effective in the other team's penalty area, left them exposed at the back.

Indeed, with just three minutes left to play, Dundee led 3–2. Lehmann had scored again and Sauzée had supplied Hibs' second goal with a trademark free kick that rocketed into the roof of the net from twenty yards out. The home side, though, had replied with three goals of their own as the Hibs defence served up a catalogue of errors. Most culpable was young left back Paul Lovering. Lovering had been a revelation since signing from Clydebank the previous season. Irrepressibly energetic and enthusiastic, he had combined hard tackling with spring-heeled aerial ability and a willingness to drive forward and support his attack. This wasn't his day, though, and he made a number of mistakes that contributed to his team staring at defeat as full time approached.

All was not lost, however. Sauzée was clearly relishing his return to big time football and he drew Hibs level with a strike from the edge of the penalty area when a corner kick was headed out to where he was hovering, ready to pounce. Hibs weren't finished yet. In added time, Lovering went some way towards making up for his earlier misfortunes by propelling a long throw into the Dundee box. When the ball broke loose, teenage substitute Kenny

Miller was on hand to volley it in to the net and seal a thrilling victory.

Miller, a Musselburgh lad, looked a tremendous prospect. The match programme for the next Hibs home game described him as a 'dyed in the wool Hibee'. The player himself was quick to play this side of things down. He admitted that he had watched Hibs regularly when he was younger but made it clear that he was more of a fan than a fanatic. At this stage of his career, though, Miller seemed to have a glittering future at Easter Road ahead of him.

The following weekend brought the first Edinburgh derby match of the new season. Hearts would visit Easter Road in a confident frame of mind, fully expecting to reinforce their status as top dogs in the capital's footballing firmament. Under Jim Jefferies, Hearts had won the Scottish Cup around the time Hibs had been bidding farewell to the Premier League. Their team contained such fine players as Gary Locke, Steven Pressley, Paul Ritchie, Gary Naysmith, Stephen Fulton, Stéphane Adam, Juanjo and ex-Hibs favourite Darren Jackson.

Hibs were in for a stern test then but their supporters welcomed this early opportunity to re-establish their side's top-flight credentials. Easter Road was all but full for the visit of Hibs' nearest neighbours and the fans in green and white, who made up the vast majority of the crowd, had plenty to cheer about in the first half. Sauzée and Latapy once again showed that they were major occasion players by commanding the play and creating opportunities for their colleagues to put Hearts under real pressure. Sauzée, in fact, was described the next day by veteran journalist Glen Gibbons as 'the coolest man on the park'. The extent of the pressure built up by Hibs is shown by the fact that three Hearts players were booked in the first forty-five minutes and Hibs were awarded a penalty. Little Latapy converted the spot kick with aplomb and Hibs would have been disappointed to go in at half time only 1–0 in front.

Unfortunately, Franck Sauzée had picked up an injury to his Achilles tendon and was unable to continue after the interval. Paul

Holsgrove took the great man's place and Hearts fought their way back into the game. A Gary McSwegan header, which looped over the head of the previously outstanding Oli Gottskalksson, gave the maroons a share of the points but Hibs could be well satisfied with their performance and reflect on how far they had come in the last twelve months.

Alex McLeish continued to tinker with his squad. He allowed Barry Lavety to return to St Mirren. Lavety was undoubtedly a talented player. He was skilful and tricky and packed a powerful shot. However, he always promised to score more goals than he actually did. This was borne out by a tally of only nine goals for Hibs in over forty matches since being signed by Alex Miller in 1996. Also on his way was David Elliot, who had been signed by Jim Duffy as a left winger but had played most often as a left back. Elliot was returning to Partick Thistle.

To balance these exits, there was also an entrance or, to be more strictly accurate, a re-entrance. Grant Brebner had been signed from Reading for a not insignificant amount of money. During his loan spell in Alex McLeish's early months at Easter Road, Brebner had done as much as anyone to try to keep Hibs in the top league. While his efforts had been in vain, he had endeared himself hugely to the Hibs support.

Brebner had been quick to point out that he, himself, was a lifelong Hibee, so when Alex Ferguson revealed that he was prepared to allow Brebner to make his move to Hibs permanent in return for an appropriate transfer fee, most Hibs fans assumed that the midfielder would soon be putting pen to paper in the Easter Road boardroom.

Then Reading came on the scene. The Berkshire club was at that time managed by the late Tommy Burns. Burns was building quite a colony of Scots at the Madejski Stadium and he offered Brebner the opportunity to join that group.

To the surprise and dismay of most Hibs supporters, Brebner agreed to sign for Reading. His popularity among the Easter Road faithful diminished overnight. The official line from Easter Road was that Brebner had opted to sign for Reading rather than Hibs because he was more familiar with the English game. Most Hibees were of the opinion that he had put money before his support for Hibs. But now, just over a year later, the lad from Danderhall had come home.

His spell with Reading had been successful. He had scored twelve goals in forty-six games and this ability to be on the score sheet regularly, when combined with his strength in the tackle and ability to pass the ball accurately over both long and short distances, marked him out as a formidable performer.

Why then, money apart, had Reading been prepared to let him go? Alex McLeish hinted at a reason in his programme notes when he wrote, 'If Grant makes the sacrifices which all good professionals must make, then he has an exciting future in the game.' McLeish was clearly implying, although no Hibs supporters were aware of it at the time, that Brebner could be side-tracked by off-field distractions.

The claim by the club that Hibs fans would be cheering all over Edinburgh on hearing of Brebner's return did not quite ring true. Most supporters were pleased to see such a potentially fine player back in green and white, but hadn't yet got over the sense of betrayal they had felt when he had turned his back on Hibs to sign for Reading. This was borne out by the greeting Brebner received from the travelling support when he made the second debut of his Hibs career against St Johnstone at McDiarmid Park. The most positive way to describe his welcome would be to call it a 'mixed reception'.

The game in Perth ended 1–1, so Hibs unbeaten start to the season continued. Alex McLeish used terminology not usually associated with football when he described his team's play as 'too pretty'. The same couldn't have been said about Mathias Jack's performance, as the big German centre half was sent off in only his fourth competitive start for Hibs. The referee who showed Jack the red card was Alan Freeland. He also booked nine players, yet the game was described in the next day's match reports as 'anything but ferocious'. Freeland was an official who didn't tend to go through matches unnoticed. During Tony Mowbray's time in charge of Hibs, Freeland sent off four players and cautioned a host of others in a match against Falkirk at Easter Road. Hibs full back David Murphy, when asked after the game if he thought that the referee had lost control, had replied, 'No, because he never had it in the first place.'

Before the St Johnstone match, Hibs had also survived an early scare in the League Cup. Buoyed by their team's attractive, attacking play in the early part of the season, a large contingent of Hibs fans had travelled to the game against Clyde. Despite goals from McGinlay and Hartley, Hibs were held to a 2–2 draw after extra time.

Hartley had scored a wonderful goal dribbling across the eighteen-yard line before swivelling to strike a rocket shot past the Clyde goalkeeper. Hartley was, of course, still playing as a winger at that time and he was a regular goal scorer. He had topped the charts with Hamilton with eleven goals in a season and when he had moved on to Raith Rovers, he had been equal top scorer alongside ex-Hibee Keith Wright with a tally of ten goals. After joining Hibs at the end of 1998, he had managed another half dozen counters before the end of the season, even though he hadn't started every game.

Alex McLeish had rung the changes for the Clyde game and had rested his big guns of Sauzée and Latapy. He was forced to bring Russell on and, after debutant Nick Colgan had saved Clyde's fourth spot kick, the little maestro coolly slotted away the winning penalty.

The fixture computer hadn't presented Hibs with the easiest of starts to the season and in their next home match, they welcomed Rangers to Easter Road. This was the Rangers team under Dick Advocaat that had been put together with no regard to cost. Rangers were really splashing the cash back then and their team had been expensively assembled. Lorenzo Amoruso, Giovanni van Bronckhorst, Jörg Albertz and Michael Mols (newly signed and scoring goals galore) had all cost £4 million. Andrei Kanchelskis had come in for £5.5 million and even full back Sergio Porrini, one of the less exalted members of their squad, had been signed for £3.2 million.

Alex McLeish missed the game as he was in hospital following minor surgery and Andy Watson, his assistant, took charge. The match turned into a duel between two Frenchmen – Franck Sauzée and the Rangers goalkeeper Lionel Charbonnier. As well as tackling ability, composure, class and the skill to pass the ball with precision and accuracy, Sauzée had brought shooting power and goals to Easter Road.

On this occasion, from a succession of shots and free kicks, he bombarded Charbonnier's goal but his countryman was up to the task as he kept them all out. The keeper was unable to hold one free kick but Shaun Dennis, following up, could only succeed in striking the rebound against the underside of the bar.

The inevitable happened. In a Rangers breakaway, Jonatan Johansson found himself in 'splendid isolation' and put the ball in the net. The linesman did not raise his flag for offside. Hibs lost 1–0 and even Rangers centre half Colin Hendry (yet another big money buy) conceded, 'We definitely rode our luck today.'

Hibs' luck didn't improve when they travelled to play Dundee United. Once again, Sauzée and Latapy were on form. Franck had a 'sizzling drive' magnificently saved by Alan Combe and Russell scored a brilliant goal after jinking round several defenders and curling the ball into the net. United, though, responded with two goals of their own, one of which was a 'once in a career wonder strike' from David Hannah before Billy Dodds sealed their victory in the last minute from a contentiously awarded penalty kick. Alex McLeish, back in harness, echoed Colin Hendry's comments of the previous week when he said, 'The luck just wasn't with us today.'

Hibs' league position now had a decidedly symmetrical look to it. After six games, they were in sixth position with six points. Their play had deserved better, though. McLeish, in fact, was happy enough with his club's start to the season to allow two more of his first team squad to leave Easter Road.

Alex Marinkov, who had been forced to play second fiddle to Mathias Jack and Shaun Dennis in the battle for the central defensive berths, returned to France. This was a shame, as

Marinkov had only been with Hibs for a few months and had looked a decent player. The announcement of his departure was slightly enigmatic, stating, 'Alex has decided his future lies outwith Scotland.' It didn't sound like the club had tried hard to persuade him otherwise.

Justin Skinner had moved to Dunfermline. Always cool and comfortable on the ball and a player capable of linking the play skilfully, Skinner had served Hibs well since joining up in Alex McLeish's early days in charge. He was popular with the fans and would be missed.

Hibs' missing luck showed no sign of returning. A Sunday home game against Kilmarnock brought an unexpected reverse. Killie were going well at that time with former Rangers duo of Ally McCoist and Ian Durrant to the fore. Two other names on the Kilmarnock team list that day have a resonance for Hibs fans. One of course was the manager Bobby Williamson, who was to play a major and, at that point, totally unforeseen part in Franck Sauzée's career path a couple of years down the line. The other was young striker Mark Roberts who, thirteen years later, was to score the goal for Second Division Ayr United that knocked Hibs out of the 2010–11 Scottish Cup.

Kilmarnock, as was typical of them under Williamson, were compact and industrious and clinical on the counter attack. Paul Hartley was booked for diving in the penalty area when television replays suggested he had been fouled, Russell Latapy was given offside when well placed to score and TV evidence showed he was clearly onside, and Dirk Lehmann rattled the underside of the bar. Killie soaked all this up and replied with three goals of their own, including one, inevitably, from McCoist. Even their manager conceded after the game that there had 'never been three goals in it'.

That was no consolation to Hibs, who now found themselves in second bottom spot in the SPL above only Aberdeen, who had lost all of their seven opening games.

5

A PREMIER PLAYER IN THE
PREMIER LEAGUE

HIBS NOW had to prepare themselves for the visit of Celtic, at that time under the stewardship of John Barnes. This was early in Barnes' reign, before Super Caley went ballistic and Celtic were in fact doing well. They should have been, too, as their side contained such high-class players as Paul Lambert, Craig Burley, the supremely talented Lubo Moravcik, Mark Viduka and that one-man goal machine Henrik Larsson.

With Celtic's potency in mind, Alex McLeish moved Franck Sauzée to sweeper. This was to be a role that Franck would occupy with distinction for Hibs in the future, of course, but on this occasion, the positional switch was purely temporary.

Franck played superbly. In fact, one Sunday newspaper described his performance as 'inspirational'. Impressive as Franck's performance was, it wasn't enough to alter the outcome of the match. Instead, the greater influence came from the contribution of referee Hugh Dallas. He sent off Sauzée and Lovering and waved away a strong penalty claim when Paul Hartley was downed in the box. Unsurprisingly, nine-man Hibs lost 2–0.

John Barnes commented after the match on the quality of Sauzée and Latapy. He described them as 'excellent players' and he was right. Big Shaun Dennis had something to say, too. Always a straight talker, he summed up the feelings of many when he said, 'We take great heart from the way we are playing. We are paying the price of being punished for almost every error, which wasn't the case at a lower level last season.'

The quality of Sauzée and Latapy gave Hibs fans comfort when they looked at the team's lowly league position. The presence of these twin talismans and the fact that Hibs continued to play good football gave the Easter Road faithful hope that things would improve for their club sooner rather than later. That is exactly what happened.

Hibs drew their next two away games at Aberdeen and Motherwell. Both matches ended 2–2 and, at Fir Park in particular, Hibs played well and deserved victory. Two significant factors in Hibs' recovery were the return to the team of Mixu Paatelainen and the introduction of Kenny Miller.

Mixu had spent time on the bench but his recall produced goals in both games, as well as bringing the experience and expertise to the team that his presence usually guaranteed. Miller brought youthful exuberance, confidence and raw talent.

Russell Latapy scored a fine goal against Motherwell (he rarely scored an ordinary one) and his consistently fine play was recognised when he was named the SPL Player of the Month. Russell's midfield comrade in arms, Sauzée, couldn't have been far behind him when the votes were counted.

A midweek blip in the League Cup, which saw Hibs lose 3–2 to Kilmarnock at Rugby Park, was put to one side as Hibs prepared for successive home games against the two Dundee clubs. Although they weren't playing badly and had started to pick up points again, Hibs were still closer to the bottom of the league than they would have wished. They lay third bottom with eight points. Victory against the two Tayside teams, then, was essential.

The Dundee match was Hibs' sixth home league fixture of the season. They still awaited their first home victory. Mind you, Hearts, Rangers and Celtic had been among the early visitors to Easter Road.

The Dundee squad contained three familiar faces. Jocky Scott, former Hibs manager and coach, Steven Tweed, a 6 feet 4 inches centre half who had walked out on Hibs to try his luck in Greek football, and Willie Miller, a hard as nails full back, who had surprised Hibs fans when he had left the club after its relegation season, would all be trying their best to put one over on their old employers.

Alex McLeish had been shuffling his pack in the SPL. Foremost First Division performers like Stuart Lovell, Stevie Crawford and Derek Collins were not featuring regularly in the starting line-up. One man who continued to hold down a place, though, was Pat McGinlay. Pat, in fact, had just played his 300th match for Hibs in the 2–2 draw at Motherwell.

Dundee took an early lead against Hibs but that was as good as it got for the Dens Parkers as they were blown away by a virtuoso Hibs display. As always, the Sauzée-Latapy axis in midfield was the fulcrum of Hibs' play. Both men were outstanding in this game and earned high praise in the press and media afterwards.

Undeterred by losing an early goal, Hibs roared back with five of their own to run out 5–2 winners. Latapy got two, including one of the solo efforts in which he seemed to specialise. Sauzée ripped a thunderous free kick beyond Rab Douglas in the Dundee goal. Also on target was young Kenny Miller, who was full of praise for his illustrious colleagues after the match.

Of Sauzée he said, 'It is unbelievable how consistently Franck hits the ball hard and accurately over both short and long distances.' He then told a story of Latapy in training where the little man had kept the ball in the air in a practice match using different parts of his body. Russell had finished his exhibition by volleying a shot into the net. According to Miller, all the players had spontaneously applauded this demonstration of skill before resuming their game.

Franck had something to say, too. He told the match programme editor, 'We are a footballing team and we proved that today.' He added, 'Russell has played at the highest level and it shows. He had a great game today.'

Sauzée himself had also played rather well. Hibs fans were starting to fully realise just how good he and Latapy were. They had taken both players to their hearts but Latapy was laid back and undemonstrative whereas Sauzée wore his heart on his sleeve. Hibs fans loved Russell but adored Franck. The wee man played and celebrated without fuss. The big man showed his whole gamut of emotions in the course of a match and celebrated his goals for Hibs with uninhibited joy. This, as well as his classy play, endeared him to the crowd.

After the Dundee match, Alex McLeish, in his normal understated way, praised Sauzée and Latapy for their 'usual creativity'. He also had a word for Grant Brebner, who had supported his two midfield partners well. Since returning to Hibs, Brebner had been quietly effective rather than outstanding but this probably had a lot to do with the company he was keeping in the centre of the park.

McLeish also announced that Stevie Crawford was being allowed to leave for Dunfermline Athletic. This split the Hibs support. Crawford was talented and popular but did tend to leave the impression that he had more to offer than he actually produced. The manager's decision to offer Dunfermline the opportunity to bring out Crawford's unfulfilled potential, rather than attempting to nurture it himself, did not meet with universal approval.

The second leg of Hibs' home double-header against the Dundee clubs was another Sky Sunday night match. Despite the game being live on television at the end of the weekend, over 11,000 fans turned up at Easter Road for the visit of Dundee United.

They witnessed a great match. Hibs won 3–2 but almost lost two points at the very end of the game. Dundee United were awarded a penalty in stoppage time and their top marksman Billy Dodds stepped up to take it. To the amazement of all and the huge relief of the home crowd, Dodds blasted his spot kick over the cross bar.

This allowed Hibs to celebrate a deserved victory. Once again, their main men had pulled the strings. Latapy had notched another two goals. As for his partner, he received the following accolade in the next day's press: 'The elegant Franck Sauzée had another wonderful match.' This was high praise indeed and thoroughly merited after yet another thoroughbred performance.

Hibs now went on to achieve a third successive league win. They went to Rugby Park and beat Kilmarnock 2–0 with young Miller scoring both goals. His second was a particularly impressive effort and his manager sung his praises. Revealing how Miller's form in the under-21 team had been 'exceptional', McLeish stated that he had had no option but to give his young striker his first team opportunity. Miller, he declared, had seized that chance with both hands.

Miller had been part of an under-21 side that was doing extremely well. They sat top of their league by the convincing margin of ten points. Strangely enough, apart from Miller, no one in that under-21 squad presided over by Donald Park was to make the breakthrough to holding down a permanent first-team place. The two who came closest were Mark Dempsie, who had a promising career ruined by injury, and Tom McManus, whose natural ability was not matched by confidence or consistent performance on the field.

Hibs' victory treble catapulted them up the league table and this was no more than their play had deserved. Since returning to the top flight, they had consistently played attacking football of good quality and had received little luck. Now their efforts were starting to gain some reward.

The brilliance of Sauzée and Latapy earned them recognition, too. As the twentieth century drew to a close, Hibs programme editor invited supporters to choose their best Hibs squad from the last hundred years. To set the ball rolling, he published his own selection. The impact already made at Easter Road by Franck and Russell was reflected by their inclusion in his group. While the editor had also predictably chosen all-time greats like Pat Stanton, Lawrie Reilly and Joe Baker, Gordon Smith, who is in the opinion of most Hibs fans, the club's greatest ever player, had been bizarrely omitted from his squad altogether.

What Hibs needed to achieve most of all was a level of consistency but this continued to elude them. A visit to Ibrox proved fruitless and the most interesting thing about a 2–0 defeat was that Hibs had now introduced Nick Colgan in goal in place of Oli Gottskalksson.

Consistency was once again eluding the big Icelander and the Irishman was given his chance. Incidentally, Rangers' goalkeeper in this game was a teenager called Mark Brown. Brown was playing because both Lionel Charbonnier and Stefan Klos were injured. He was to end up with Hibs, of course, although he did spend time with the other half of the Old Firm en route to Easter Road.

Rangers' first goal came from Jonatan Johansson. Left winger Neil McCann laid on a perfect cross for the goal, just as he had done for his colleague Don Hutchison a few days earlier as Scotland had beaten England at Wembley. McCann, of course, is now a television pundit but he showed that he still had something to offer on the field early in 2011 when he returned to play for Dundee on a short-term basis and scored the winning goal in his first game. Johansson was later to join Hibs but he proved to be much less potent in a green jersey than he had been in a blue one.

Jorg Albertz scored Rangers' second goal with a trademark free kick. Rangers were bursting with star-studded names like Albertz back then and Ibrox seemed to be awash with money. This was in contrast to Easter Road, where in the match programme leading up to Christmas, Hibs exhorted their young supporters to enter a competition to produce a card on the theme 'A Hibee Christmas'. The prize to encourage a large number of entries was neither health conscious nor overly generous; it was a giant Toblerone bar!

If the Ibrox reverse was expected, Hibs next defeat was certainly not. St Johnstone came to Easter Road for a Wednesday night fixture and caught Hibs on a bad night. The Perth side left with a deserved 1–0 victory as Hibs failed totally to get to grips with a match that they should have been capable of winning comfortably. Alex McLeish described his team as lacklustre. He was being kind. Mixu Paatelainen hit the nail on the head when he said, 'We did not pass the ball. We simply lumped it up the park.'

These back-to-back defeats undid a lot of Hibs' earlier good work and it was time for the club to get back on the rails. This was achieved in the next home game against Aberdeen. In the Dons goal was forty-one-year-old Jim Leighton. Jim had been a magnificent goalkeeper for Hibs before returning to Pittodrie and his form there had been good enough for him to have represented Scotland in the World Cup Finals in France just a year earlier. On this occasion, his old colleagues beat him twice without reply. Leighton could only push out a Franck Sauzée special and Paatelainen buried the rebound. Pat McGinlay added a second. Both McGinlay and Paatelainen had scored far fewer goals thus far in the SPL than they had in the First Division, so it was encouraging to see them back on target.

John Hughes was back in central defence again after a spell out with injury and he teamed up in that area once more with his old partner Shaun Dennis. His manager was pleased with his contribution. McLeish said, 'We lost two soft goals against Rangers but the return of the club captain gave us some steel.'

McLeish added a third central defender to his back line for Hibs' next match, the visit to Parkhead to play Celtic. Mathias Jack joined Hughes and Dennis in an obvious attempt to stifle Celtic's wide range of attacking options. It worked until Celtic were awarded and converted a penalty. After that, it was one sided and Celtic ran out comfortable 4–0 winners.

Franck Sauzée missed the Parkhead match through injury and Hibs certainly missed him. Franck was now thirty-four years old but playing as well as ever. He returned for the home game against Motherwell and his influence was there for all to see. The only phrase to describe this match accurately belonged to Franck's native tongue. For the third time in five months, Hibs outplayed Well but had to settle for a 2–2 draw. The game had 'déjà vu' written all over it.

Paatelainen and McGinlay continued their return to scoring form with the Hibs goals. Mixu once again followed in on a rebound from a Sauzée strike and Pat pulled off a stunning overhead kick. John Spencer induced a feeling of both injustice and familiarity when he equalised for Motherwell in the very last minute of the match.

Hibs' next match had enormous significance. They were going to Tynecastle to play Hearts in the last Edinburgh derby match of the twentieth century. The game was keenly anticipated and was being widely referred to as the Millennium Derby.

Alan Bennett, the author and playwright, once described history as 'just one bloody thing after another'. Hibs fans could have applied that description to derby matches in recent years if they had substituted the word 'defeat' for the word 'thing'.

Under Alex Miller, Hibs had been woeful in games against their city rivals, infamously going a mind blowing twenty-two matches without a win in the fixture. Miller's successor, Jim Duffy, had started with a 4–0 home defeat against the old enemy, so he hadn't exactly bucked the trend.

Under McLeish, though, things had improved. In his first derby, Hearts challenging for the league title at the time, had been beaten on a snowy April afternoon at Easter Road, thanks to two wonder strikes from Barry Lavety and Kevin Harper. On Hibs' return to the SPL, they had had the better of a 1–1 draw at Easter Road in August. However, Tynecastle was seen as a derby day fortress for Hearts, so any optimism going into the Millennium match-up was definitely of the guarded variety.

One difference from most recent capital confrontations, though, was the presence of Sauzée and Latapy in the green and white of Hibernian. Russell had been through a quiet spell of form and was surely overdue a return to his best. Franck, for his part, had been commanding and inspirational for most of the season. Both of these outstanding players relished the bigger games.

As Sunday, 19 December, and the Millennium Derby approached, the big question down Easter Road way was, 'Will it be business as usual on the derby front or can Sauzée and Latapy inspire Hibs to something special?'

6

MILLENNIUM MAGIC

IT IS LIKELY that Hearts supporters travelled to Tynecastle for the Millennium Derby in a much more confident frame of mind than their counterparts from across the city. Since returning to the SPL, Hibs' performances had lacked consistency and they had been unable to sustain their better form for more than two or three games at a time. Hearts, on the other hand, had, under the management of Jim Jefferies, been at the forefront of Scottish football for quite some time. Coming into the derby, they had been further boosted by significant investment from the Scottish Media Group. This had enabled Jefferies to add to his playing squad and, in the lead-up to the last capital clash of the twentieth century, he had done exactly that. He had procured goalkeeper Antti Niemi, centre half Gordan Petric and midfielder Fitzroy Simpson. These acquisitions made a strong Hearts team stronger still.

Despite the pre-match portents being less than positive, the Hibs players travelled to the game in good spirits. The mood on their coach as they crossed Edinburgh was relaxed and light hearted but, as Franck Sauzée recalled, this all changed when they got into the dressing room at Tynecastle. Then captain John Hughes took a hand. The skipper used his motivational powers to the full as he impressed on his team mates how much this game meant and exhorted them to give their all to win it. As Sauzée put it, 'All of a sudden everything was very emotional and highly charged.'

Hughes continued to urge his team mates on as they waited in the tunnel before taking the field. When the players did run out onto the pitch, they found it to be in excellent condition despite sub-zero air temperatures. They also discovered what one newspaper described the next day as a 'sensational atmosphere'.

Hibs delighted their support, packed as always into the school end of the ground, with a fine start. They were cool and commanding and looking at ease in their intimidating surroundings. By half time, the greens were two goals ahead.

First Russell Latapy teed Dirk Lehmann up for a low, well-struck shot into Niemi's net from the edge of the penalty area. Lehmann's selection in front of nineteen-year-old Kenny Miller had been a surprise. Miller had, after all, scored six goals in nine starts. His omission was a disappointment for the Chelsea scout in the stand who had travelled all the way from London to watch him. It also came as a shock to the massed Hibs support. However, Alex McLeish had been proved correct by this excellent opening goal from the German striker.

There was even better to come. When Brebner crossed the ball into the Hearts penalty area, Steven Pressley could only clear it as far as Franck Sauzée, who was twenty-five yards from goal. Sauzée roared to Stuart Lovell, in close proximity, to leave the ball and then, without breaking stride, struck it perfectly into the corner of the Hearts goal. The shot was unstoppable and so was Franck. He raced off in triumph to celebrate with the Hibs crowd at the other end of the ground. He must have run seventy-five yards, with Yogi Hughes in close pursuit, before standing in front of his adoring supporters to treasure the moment. Many Hibs fans are of the opinion that this was the furthest and fastest that Franck ran in all his time at Easter Road!

Stuart Lovell, now restored to the team and playing well, remembers the goal clearly. 'I was close to the ball and thinking about hitting it. When I heard Franck's shout, I got out of the way and thank God I did. I could never have struck the ball as sweetly as Franck did. I knew it was a goal from the moment it left his foot.'

Another well known Hibee with fond memories of Sauzée's supersonic strike is author and historian John Campbell. John recalls, 'I watched that game from the Tynecastle Press Box where I was covering it for the Hibs website. The Press Box itself sits right in front of the Directors Box and is pretty well surrounded by Hearts fans and so, as each goal went in and I turned to grin at fellow Hibee and journalist Simon Pia who was sitting near me, I felt I was glowing green in a sea of maroon. At the end of the game, I turned to face the Directors Box and couldn't help but smile as I watched the glum home directors shaking hands with their restrained but clearly delighted Easter Road counterparts. It was a night to remember and it was a night when one solitary act etched itself into my brain, and that was the sight of Franck crashing home a glorious long-range drive before turning tail and rushing to the opposite end to celebrate with several thousand delirious Hibees, for truly he was one of them.'

This goal and the celebration that followed it have become iconic Hibernian images. After the game, Sauzée said, 'It was like a big party. I knew how much it meant to the fans.' It meant the world but there was still more than half the match to go and nothing was decided yet.

Predictably, Jim Jefferies sent his team out for the second half in a fired up state and unsurprisingly, Hearts stormed the Hibs goal. Nick Colgan, in his first derby and a seminal one at that, stood firm and made a number of fine saves. This, in fact, was probably Colgan's best game in a Hibs jersey. He was helped out by Sauzée on one occasion, though. Stuart Lovell still marvels at what happened. 'Nick saved a shot from Scott Severin. Andy Kirk was about to pounce on the rebound. I was going to shell the ball into the stand when Franck appeared on the scene. He nutmegged Kirk and passed the ball out to a team mate. My heart was in my mouth for a second but I needn't have worried as Franck was in complete control of the situation. The Hibs fans behind the goal roared their approval of Franck's cheek and I thought to myself, my God that guy has got so much class and composure.'

Having weathered the storm, Hibs once again began to carve out chances of their own. Russell Latapy went close on three occasions. Sauzée was running the show. As the *Daily Record* put it the next day: 'Sauzée was the controller of the middle of the field and he produced a gem of a pass to release Latapy.' The little Trinidadian nutmegged Petric but was denied by Niemi. Russell then sent a great drive and an impudent chip inches wide of the target.

A third goal did come, though. Pat McGinlay and Kenny Miller had come on as substitutes and they both played their part. McGinlay headed forward a weak clearance from Niemi and Miller fastened on to the ball to draw the goalkeeper and use his left foot to place the ball into the corner of the net with the aplomb of a veteran.

The final whistle signalled mass jubilation at the Hibs end of the stadium. Captain Hughes led his men to the fans and led the celebrations when they got there. All of the team had played their part. The impressive Colgan in goal, resourceful full backs Collins and Smith, the defiant captain and his rock solid central defensive partner Shaun Dennis, the enterprising Stuart Lovell and Grant Brebner in midfield, and the ever dangerous Lehmann and Paatelainen up front had all excelled.

Substitutes McGinlay, Miller and Bannerman had played their part, too. The undoubted star men, though, were inevitably Franck Sauzée and Russell Latapy.

Both men paid tribute to their skipper. Sauzée said, 'John Hughes showed unbelievable passion and motivation before the game. He was like a man going to war.' Latapy added, 'Yogi changed the mentality of the dressing room.'

Nick Colgan remembers the game well. 'The Millennium Derby is probably my favourite game for Hibs. I had a less than ideal preparation for the match. I got the keys for our new house in Peebles that day and then I had to go out to the airport to pick up my wife, mother-in-law and baby son. I was a bit fraught by the time I joined up with the boys. I felt really nervous at the start of the game but I settled down and, thankfully, played really well. Franck's goal was unforgettable and our fans were unbelievable. We knew exactly how much beating Hearts meant to them, as Yogi had drummed that into us. Our dressing room was brilliant afterwards and it was a fantastic feeling to have beaten our greatest rivals on such a landmark occasion.'

Describing the magical mood that prevailed during the game, Sauzée had this to say: 'There was something special about this night. All of the stadium was quiet except for the one end with our fans, which was unbelievable. It was a strange atmosphere but a great sensation.'

The Frenchman revealed how intense the days leading up to the game had been. He said, 'Everywhere I went, the fans shouted to me, "Franck, you have to win the derby."'

After this victory, Hibs supporters stopped Sauzée in the street or shouted to him from their cars, 'Hey Frankie boy, we did it!'

In his pre-match team talk at Tynecastle, Alex McLeish had told his players, 'Give the ball to Franck and Russell.' They had done exactly that and it had paid dividends. After the match, McLeish thanked the Hibs supporters for their 'phenomenal backing'. Hibs chairman Malcolm McPherson had words of appreciation for his manager. He wrote in the next match programme, 'Alex McLeish's affection for our club comes from the passion that he has found in the support. There is no doubt that he has a burning desire to be successful at Easter Road while playing a style of football that the Hibernian supporters rightly expect.'

While longer-term success remained a future goal, there was no doubt that winning this landmark Edinburgh derby meant a great deal to the manager and the club's supporters.

McLeish reflected on the lack of conviction shown in the recent visits by Hibs to Ibrox and Parkhead and compared this with the belief shown at Tynecastle. He declared, 'It was fantastic to see our supporters so happy. The significance of winning the last derby of the twentieth century added spice to the occasion.'

Two major players in the match had risen from their sick beds to take part. Dirk Lehmann shrugged off a temperature to score the first goal while Hearts manager Jim Jefferies defied a bout of the flu to take his usual place in the technical area. He probably wished that he had stayed in his bed.

The press and media were quick to praise Hibs and put this famous victory in context. The *Daily Record* confirmed that this had been Hibs' biggest victory at Tynecastle since the famous 7–0 thrashing of 1973. It added, 'Hearts were outplayed, out thought and outclassed. They were humiliated by their greatest rivals on their own patch.' This was the sweetest of music to Hibernian ears. Stuart Lovell and Kenny Miller went out for a quiet drink after the match. They could hardly believe it when Hearts supporters came up to them and congratulated them on their performance. 'I suppose that just goes to show how well we had played,' reflects Lovell when he turns his mind back to that night.

BBC Scotland's Richard Gordon was certainly impressed by Hibs' performance when he said, 'It is all smiles at Easter Road tonight. Sauzée and Latapy were dominant.' Hibs' match programme added, 'Nowhere was Hibs dominance more pronounced than in midfield where, once again, Hibernian exuded class.' That class was supplied, in the main, by the little magician from Trinidad and, most notably, the artist from Aubenas, the man of the match, Franck Sauzée.

Sauzée's goal celebration at Tynecastle summed up the rapport that now existed between the midfield maestro and his supporters. This was, undoubtedly, a mutual love affair. Jonathan Swift once wrote, 'Who'er excels in what we prize, appears a hero in our eyes.' He might have been writing about Franck Sauzée and the Hibernian support.

At the last Hibs v Hearts match of the twentieth century, there had been 17,954 fans in attendance. The majority had been bedecked in maroon. The 3,500 wearing green and white, however, had been part of an unforgettable experience. Their team had made history and as one millennium prepared to give way to the next, Hibernian

FC sat in fifth position in the Scottish Premier League, four points in front of the men of Heart of Midlothian. Incidentally, for those with an interest in history, the very first derby of the twentieth century had ended in a 3–3 draw.

Hibs' first match after their Tynecastle triumph, their final game of the millennium, also ended in a draw as Kilmarnock came to Easter Road between Christmas and New Year and once more caused Hibs problems. Indeed, it took late goals from Mixu Paatelainen and Kenny Miller, again on as a substitute, to earn a share of the points.

The SPL then went into cold storage for a couple of weeks as the clubs enjoyed the winter break that was in operation at that time. Hibs enjoyed theirs more than most as they travelled to Russell Latapy's homeland of Trinidad and Tobago, where they had what Mixu Paatelainen called a 'mini pre-season'. Hibs played two matches on the islands, won them both with Latapy on target each time and brought a couple of local players back with them to have a trial period at the club.

Hibs kept up their drawing habit when they got back to league business. Without the injured Franck Sauzée, they fought out a goalless match with Dundee United at Tannadice. Sauzée's replacement was a young debutant called Ian Murray. John Rowbotham, the referee, turned down a strong penalty claim, which Alex McLeish reckoned looked like a spot kick from where he was sitting.

Now it was Scottish Cup time. This, of course, is the time of the season when Hibs supporters allow themselves to dream that this will be their year. Reality usually shatters that dream pretty quickly. In 2000, Hibs' manager was sharing the fans' optimism. He declared, 'The cup is high on my priority list.' It is probably fair to say that it was right at the very top of every supporter's priority list.

Hibs were drawn at home to Dunfermline in the third round. The Pars squad was full of well known names. In goal was Ian Westwater, formerly of Hearts and soon to be Hibs' goalkeeping coach. Eddie May, an ex-Hibee and future Falkirk manager, was in midfield and was joined there by former Rangers enforcer, Ian Ferguson. Up front were future Bolton manager Owen Coyle and a young centre forward called Colin Nish!

Hibs had a comfortable passage. Kenny Miller, in from the start this time, was on target in sixty-five seconds. Goals from Grant Brebner (his first since returning to Easter Road), young Murray and Derek Collins helped to seal a convincing 4–1 victory.

The crowd was a healthy 10,863. Mind you, that figure was way below Hibs' record Scottish Cup attendance, which was a staggering 143,000 for a semi-final match against Rangers at Hampden in 1948. Most fans left the ground thinking that, on current form, their team might well go beyond the semi-final stage this time around. This view was shared by the BBC Radio Scotland pundit, Gordon Smith, who stated, 'If Hibs continue to play like this, they must be in with a great chance of going all the way in this competition.'

One team that wouldn't be going any further in the 1999–2000 Scottish Cup was Celtic, who had suffered a famous defeat to Inverness Caley Thistle. Hearts had almost followed Celtic out of the cup but had managed to recover from being 2–0 down to Stenhousemuir to squeeze through 3–2.

It was a time of change at Easter Road as the club eschewed its old badge, which had never been popular with its support, and introduced a new one, which had been designed by a teenage fan called Bryan Leslie. Bryan's design showcased the harp to denote Hibs' Irish roots, a ship to mark their base in the port of Leith and a castle to provide the connection with Edinburgh. The new crest met with almost universal approval.

Franck Sauzée was indulging in a bit of change as well. Franck had changed his hair colour a couple of times since joining Hibs (he had even gone for a blond look on one occasion) and now changed the colour of the gloves he wore on cold match days from black to Hibernian green. The supporters liked this and wondered if the Sauzée thatch would be next for the green look!

A feature on Franck at this time was entitled 'Franck Sauzée: The man who has won Hibs Hearts'. That was clever and also one hundred per cent true. In the article, Franck told of how he preferred playing to training. As he put it himself, 'I live for the Saturdays.'

Franck played next on a Sunday as Hibs were once again live on Sky on a Sunday evening when Rangers came to call. A fine match ended 2–2 as Hibs continued their sequence of draws in the league. On fire striker Kenny Miller got both goals. The second was from an exquisite Sauzée pass. This put Hibs 2–1 in front but a late Neil McCann goal rescued a point for Rangers, who were far and away the strongest team in Scotland at that point. Nick Colgan got a hand to McCann's shot but couldn't stop it from entering his net.

A photograph of the Hibs players celebrating Miller's second goal demonstrates clearly why the Hibs fans loved Franck Sauzée so much. Sauzée is in the middle of the group of team mates congratulating Miller and his whole face is a picture of pleasure. The other players look happy but Sauzée is lit up with joy. The fact that he cared so much is what endeared him to his supporters.

He earned more praise, along with Russell Latapy, from Hibs centre half, Mathias Jack. Making the point that Scottish football was much faster than the style of play he was used to in Germany, Jack said, 'The game in Scotland is on fire. The pace just never slackens. Hibs are different, though, because we have two playmakers in Franck and Russell.'

Hibs also had two new signings. Centre half Martin McIntosh, who had arrived from Stockport County, and Caribbean forward Earl Jean, who had signed on until the end of the season. Fabrice Henry, on the other hand, had left Easter Road. Things had not worked out for Sauzée's compatriot and he had gone back to France.

Two new faces were making a name for themselves in Hibs' under-18 team. They were strikers and they were banging in the goals. Hibs then Director of Youth Development, John Park, was predicting a bright future for both lads. He was to be proved correct, as the players in question, Garry O'Connor and Derek Riordan, haven't really stopped scoring goals since.

Next up in the Scottish Cup for Hibs was what looked like a very winnable home tie with Clydebank. A well known face in the Bankies ranks was Greg Miller, son of former Easter Road manager Alex Miller. Miller had signed both his sons for Hibs but neither of them had managed to win a regular first team place, and both had ended up playing their football in the lower divisions.

John Rowbotham was again the referee and he sent off Hibs' Tom Smith for aiming a kick at Miller. Smith missed but the referee didn't miss his action and he had to go. Things got worse when Clydebank took the lead from the penalty spot. The spot kick was awarded for a handball that most people considered accidental. Rowbotham saw it differently, though, and Hibs were in trouble. The ten men salvaged a draw and a replay, however, when Franck Sauzée sent Paul Hartley clear with a superbly judged pass. Hartley finished coolly.

Russell Latapy was away on Gold Cup duty with Trinidad and Tobago and both he and Sauzée were absentees when Hibs travelled to Perth for a league game. It was a bad night for McLeish's men. They missed a host of chances and were on the receiving end of another dubious penalty award. Nick Colgan was adjudged to have caught John Paul McBride when the goalkeeper was adamant that he had made clean contact with the ball. The resultant goal was enough to win the game for St Johnstone, much to Alex McLeish's disappointment. His post-match verdict was, 'We definitely didn't deserve to lose that game.'

Stuart Lovell had acknowledged in a recent interview that Sauzée and Latapy were the main men at Easter Road. He had made the point, though, that the rest of the Hibs team had to get the ball to them. According to Lovell, this made him and his colleagues 'unsung heroes'. This may have been so but there was no doubt that when Franck and Russell were missing, as had been the case at McDiarmid Park, Hibs were nothing like as potent.

Even Alex McLeish would have had to admit that Hibs deserved to lose their next match, a disappointing 4–0 reverse at Pittodrie. Aberdeen had rallied after their early season difficulties and were now just five points behind Hibs. Two successive defeats had seen Hibs go from fifth top of the ten-team SPL to a position close to the bottom of the division. Those who are currently promoting the return of a league of this size should bear in mind that such a small number of clubs in a division inevitably leads to no side outwith the Old Firm being far from the relegation zone at any given time.

Hibs bounced back in style, though, in their next home game, which was in their favourite Sunday night live Sky Television slot. The visitors were Celtic, now under the management of Kenny Dalglish after John Barnes' enforced departure, and the Hibees were brilliant. They won 2–1 with goals from Pat McGinlay and that man Kenny Miller once again. A Sauzée free kick led to Miller's goal.

Once again, the big occasion brought out the best in Sauzée. He was named as man of the match and extracts from the reports in the Monday newspapers show why. 'Sauzée orchestrated a stunning move with a tremendous piece of skill,' said one. Another added, 'Franck Sauzée is only a few months away from the end of a glittering career, which is a crying shame for those who love to see the game played properly.' Franck had announced that he would retire at the end of the season – a decision that had saddened all Hibs supporters. For the moment, though, they were content to dwell in the present and revel in the great man's performances.

Franck had been paid an indirect compliment in the match programme. The editor had recalled George Best's last game for Hibs, which had been a 2–0 win over Falkirk. He described Best's performance as thus, 'George displayed close control, dribbling skills and shooting power of which Franck Sauzée would have been proud.' Praise indeed! Celtic manager Dalglish was also handing out praise. He said, 'Hibs played very well and we did not cope with them.'

Hibs were delighted to welcome back Russell Latapy for their next match, the cup replay with Clydebank. The replay proved much more comfortable than the original tie had done. Stuart

Lovell got his first goal of the season and Dirk Lehmann and Franck Sauzée notched their first strikes of the new millennium as Hibs ran out easy 3–0 winners. Sauzée's goal was a twenty-yard rocket.

Things were looking good down Easter Road way. Hibs had their two best players available again and they were in the Scottish Cup quarter final. They also had the prospect of a home derby against Hearts to look forward to. It would be nice to follow up the famous win in the Millennium fixture with another victory on home soil and that is exactly what Alex McLeish and his team intended to do.

7

A BLOOD-STAINED HERO

BEFORE TURNING their minds to the imminent third derby match of the season, Hibs had to focus on Scottish Cup business once more. A third successive home draw against lower league opposition saw Falkirk visit Easter Road. The Bairns were never likely to be a pushover and so it proved. They tested Hibs to the full and a last-minute Pat McGinlay goal made the 3–1 score line look more comfortable than it had actually been. Franck Sauzée had been at his 'prompting best' and his midfield partner Russell Latapy had weighed in with two goals. In truth, though, Hibs had been forced to work very hard for their victory. As Russell said, 'We ground out a result but the most important thing is that we are now in the semi-final of the Scottish Cup.'

Franck had something to say, too. Reflecting on his two French Cup winner's medals and his prized European Cup win, he reflected, 'I find it hard to believe that a team like Hibs hasn't won the Scottish Cup since 1902. Maybe we can change that this year.'

That view was shared not only by the 13,551 fans who had attended the Falkirk match, but also by many other Hibs supporters and sympathisers who were beginning to allow themselves to think that this might just be the year when what for so long had seemed like the impossible dream finally came true.

First, though, there was a derby day date with Hearts. Going into the match, new signing Martin McIntosh commented that even in

England, where he had been playing until recently, players and supporters had been talking about the Sauzée-Latapy partnership at Hibs. Every Hibs supporter was hoping that the partnership would be at its most productive when Hearts crossed the city to Easter Road.

Although Franck and Russell were very different players, they had class and abundant skill in common. The little Trinidadian magician would pick the ball up at half way and run at defenders. He would dribble past them or pick out a slide-rule pass. When he wasn't making goals for others, he was scoring them himself. He wasn't one for chasing back, though, and could have quiet games or quiet periods in games even when he was on form.

Sauzée was rarely out of the game. He supported his defence, sprayed passes from midfield and got forward to score. He was the more complete player of Easter Road's dynamic duo. Hibs had beaten Celtic without Latapy but they might not have beaten them without Sauzée.

Hibs fans, however, were not too concerned with making comparisons between their two superstars. They were more interested in enjoying what they brought to their club. Supporters of Hibs were raised on stories of great teams and players of the past. Whether it was the Famous Five, Joe Baker, Willie Hamilton or the Turnbull's Tornadoes side of the 1970s they were hearing about, followers of Hibernian got the message loud and clear. That message was unequivocal and it stated that their team should play with flair. That hadn't been the case for almost twenty years now. Under Alex Miller, Hibs had won a trophy and had fine players like Keith Wright and Darren Jackson up front, and Kevin McAllister and Michael O'Neill out wide. Despite the presence of these excellent attackers, Hibs had still played with industry rather than inspiration in the central midfield area.

Now style and swagger was back and a Hibs team, which had been relegated less than two years earlier, was strutting its stuff in a very impressive fashion indeed. The combination of Sauzée and

Latapy, whose silky skills complemented each other perfectly, was at the heart of this revival.

The visit of Hearts in March 2000 was keenly anticipated on the east side of Edinburgh. Painful memories of Hearts' twenty-two games in a row run without defeat in derby matches were starting to recede. Hibs had won two and drawn two of the last four derbies and Alex McLeish had an unbeaten record in the fixture.

Things didn't start well, though, as former Hibs favourite Darren Jackson, who had arrived at Tynecastle via Celtic, put Hearts in front with a tremendous, early left-foot drive. This was as good as it got for Hearts, though. Driven on by Sauzée and with Latapy at his twinkling best, Hibs overran their neighbours.

The two combined for Hibs' first goal. Sauzée made a diagonal run and took a number of Hearts defenders with him. This created a gap into which Latapy could carry the ball and he needed no second invitation. Moving across the penalty area from left to right, he showed great close control before bulleting a shot low past Antti Niemi.

It was Sauzée's turn next. Left back Tom Smith, a steady performer when his regular injury problems allowed him to play, sent a high cross to the far post. Sauzée jumped with a couple of Hearts defenders. He must have known that he was liable to suffer a clash of heads but, showing great courage and leaping massively, he directed a magnificent looping header over Niemi into the corner of the Hearts net.

As he met the ball, Franck suffered the inevitable collision with the back of his opponent's head. He fell in a heap and the cheers of the Hibs support stilled to apprehensive silence. Franck received treatment for some time and then got gingerly to his feet, holding a blood-stained handkerchief to his mouth. He had lost four teeth but had made it clear to the physio that he had no intention of leaving the field. As Franck trotted back to the centre circle, the fans began to sing 'Sauzée, there's only one Sauzée'. He waved his handkerchief to the crowd in acknowledgement. It was another great Franck Sauzée Hibernian moment.

When Franck reflected on his brave and brilliant goal after the match, he had this to say: 'Hibs fans have impressed me. They are incredible and it's important when you play for a club to have a rapport like that. The goal against Hearts – I watched the ball coming across. I saw it looping towards me. I was aware of the fans and the atmosphere. It was a motivation to me. I was able to run and put my head on the ball because I could hear the fans. When you hear the fans like that you feel you have to win.'

Hibs were determined to win and weren't finished yet. Next, Latapy went at the Hearts defence. He jinked this way and that and left a trail of defenders in his wake. Niemi parried his shot but the ball broke to Mixu Paatelainen, who made the game safe from close range.

The way Russell had toyed with the Hearts defence and given them problems with retaining their balance as he changed direction with bewildering speed recalled the reaction of Emlyn Hughes, the stalwart Liverpool and England defender, after being given a chasing by Jimmy Johnstone at Hampden. Hughes had summed up the runaround he had received by saying, 'I felt like I had twisted blood.' That's how the Hearts players must have felt after trying to cope with the trickery of Russell Latapy.

The man of the match once more, though, in Hibs 3–1 victory was Franck Sauzée. Again the press sung his praise. Tributes included: 'Sauzée was at his mercurial best. He brought a touch of class and calm to a match which was played at a frenetic pace. Hibs fans should start a pressure group to persuade him not to retire,' and, 'Sauzée has a repertoire almost unmatched in Scottish football.'

Hibs supporters wondered why the writer had thought it necessary to insert the word 'almost' before 'unmatched'. In their opinion, no one compared with Sauzée. Alex McLeish agreed. 'Franck had a wonderful game. I don't know how I will replace the man. To get someone of the same quality at the same age would cost me millions and I don't have millions.'

Captain John Hughes, who had produced another magnificent derby performance, had his say as well. 'Franck does things that the rest of us can only dream of. Now he's lost his four front teeth and that will make him a folk hero in Leith.'

Nick Colgan was also impressed by the inspirational Frenchman's courage. He said, 'When Franck didn't get up right away after heading his goal, I knew that it was a bad one, as he didn't normally stay down. After the game, with his usual modesty, he told us, "This won't do much for my looks but there, again, I wasn't the best looking man to begin with." I am sure that there are a lot of ladies out there who would have disagreed with that statement.'

Sauzée himself, no doubt speaking out of a very sore mouth, said, 'I would lose my teeth again if it meant scoring for Hibs in a derby.' No wonder the fans loved him.

Alex McLeish also took time out to praise the players in his team whom Stuart Lovell had christened the 'unsung heroes'. Mentioning Derek Collins, Tom Smith, Lovell himself, Pat McGinlay and Mixu Paatelainen by name, he stressed the valuable contribution that they had made. However, he added, 'The difference Sauzée and Latapy bring to our team is often the main factor in big games and that was the case again on Saturday.'

One of the qualities that Franck and Russell had was experience. Franck's English was improving now as he and his wife Guylaine had been receiving regular language lessons. He was able to make the following insightful point: 'In France, experience is a pejorative. This is not the case in Scotland. With experience, you can talk to other players and help them. You can also take the ball on and change the game.'

Alex McLeish's derby record now looked even better. He recently reflected on what had been the secret of his success in matches against Hearts during his time as a manager of Hibs. Alex explained, 'From the minute I walked into Easter Road, I tried to convey to my players that they should not fear or be fazed by any opposition. That was exactly the approach which had been drilled into me during my time as a player at Aberdeen when we won everything going. Players who can adopt this mind set, prosper. Those who can't, fall by the wayside.'

As had been the case throughout the season, Hibs followed a couple of good performances with disappointing displays. After the outstanding win over Hearts, they lost at home to Dundee (Sauzée missed the game after repair work to his injured mouth) and away to Kilmarnock. This prompted their manager to declare, 'I want consistency.' That is exactly what his club's supporters wanted, too.

As the Scottish Cup semi-final approached, Hibs had to recover their best form. The draw had again been kind, pairing the Hibees with Aberdeen, a team twelve points below them in the league. Rangers looked the likeliest opponents in the final and Hibs had everything to play for.

The last game before the trip to Hampden to face the Dons was a home match against Dundee United and Hibs got back on the victory trail. Paul Hartley was restored to the team just twenty-four hours after turning down a transfer to Tannadice and, in the way that fate so often operates in football, he scored the only goal of the game. Hartley revealed afterwards that his manager had said to him before the game, 'Go out and show them what they are missing.' He did exactly that.

Derek Collins, Franck Sauzée and Martin McIntosh had all gone off injured at half time against Dundee United but all managed to take their places in Hibs' starting line-up for the semi-final.

In the build up to the match, Sauzée had given Hibs supporters the news they wanted to hear. He announced that he had set aside his retirement plans and signed a new one-year contract. There was joy around Easter Road at this marvellous news.

Franck said, 'I love life in Edinburgh with my wife and everyone at Hibs. It is like a dream. The support of the fans and the players is what convinced me to shelve my retirement plans and sign a new contract. I would love to put Hibs into the Scottish Cup Final.' He revealed that Russell Latapy, Mixu Paatelainen and Pat McGinlay, among others, had urged him to keep playing. The Hibs support, too, had taken every opportunity to appeal to him to extend his career. All of this attention and affection had, said Sauzée in his own inimitable way, 'struck me in the heart'.

Alex McLeish was delighted. He said, 'Franck has been overwhelmed with the support of the fans over the last few months. His family is happy here and his legs are still strong, so he decided to carry on. When we knew that he was prepared to stay, we wasted no time in signing him up again.'

This was a massive boost and Hibs supporters were so keen to cheer on their team at Hampden that the club had to ask for an extra allocation of tickets. Over 22,000 travelled to Glasgow to watch a Sunday evening match, which was being shown live on Sky Television. Around three quarters of that number were bedecked in green and white.

The first half of the semi-final was cagey and Hibs suffered a blow when Derek Collins went off injured with a recurrence of his hamstring injury. This necessitated a reshuffle, which saw Stuart Lovell switch to right back and Paul Hartley come on. This did not help Hibs' team shape and Alex McLeish was disappointed that Collins had declared himself fit to play when he hadn't fully recovered from the strain he had picked up in the previous match.

The game, and Hibs, improved in the second half. Little Latapy showed mesmerising skill to run from half way and shoot past Jim Leighton to put Hibs ahead. Instead of building on this foundation to go on and win the game convincingly, however, the greens unaccountably sat back in defence. They stopped passing the ball and began to clear it aimlessly. This gifted Aberdeen possession and the inevitable happened.

First Arild Stavrum equalised, then Andy Dow put the Dons ahead. Former Hibee Dow's goal was a stunning right-foot volley. He normally used that foot only for standing on. As Nick Colgan said after the match, 'When Andy Dow scores with his right foot, you know it's not your night.'

Hibs launched a late rally but, in truth, didn't look like equalising. This defeat was a huge disappointment.

Captain John Hughes said, 'I was in tears for the last five minutes of the game. I sensed that we weren't going to manage to score and I knew that I wasn't going to get that open-top bus ride down Leith Walk with the cup.'

Alex McLeish declared, 'That was a sore one. To see and hear that fantastic Hibernian support was a wonderful experience. You did the club proud and I am absolutely gutted that we couldn't steer the club to a European place and a cup final. I won't rest until we get to a cup final.'

Russell Latapy, whose magnificent goal had proved to be in vain, also had words for the supporters. He said, 'The fans were magnificent. They deserve us to be in the final and I am really disappointed for them.'

Franck Sauzée had just been made SPL Player of the Month but that was little consolation for him or his club's followers. Hibees everywhere were truly depressed at the passing up of what had appeared to be a golden opportunity to bring the Scottish Cup back to Easter Road at last.

Unsurprisingly, the rest of Hibs' season fizzled out in anti-climax. There was one more win, in the last home game of the season against Aberdeen, and draws with Celtic and St Johnstone. The last four matches of the campaign were all away fixtures and Hibs lost the lot, including a 2–1 defeat at Tynecastle, Alex McLeish's first derby defeat.

Two things stood out in the match against Celtic. Earl Jean, who had disappeared from the scene after signing for Hibs in January, re-emerged on the bench at Parkhead. He was never seen again! Much more significantly, Mathias Jack, who had lost his place in central defence, was given a run as a holding player in central midfield. This proved to be a McLeish masterstroke and the big man's combination of strength and skill was to prove vital in season 2000–01.

Stuart Lovell gave Hibs the lead at Celtic Park and the home team was flattered by its late equaliser. As Alex McLeish put it, 'When you come to Parkhead and are disappointed with only taking one point, then you are talking my type of language.'

McLeish was under no illusions, though, that his team was the finished article. During the last home match of the season, won thanks to Kenny Miller's tenth league goal of the season, a fan shouted at the manager, 'McLeish, this is rubbish.' The big man replied, 'I know.'

As season 1999–2000 came to an end, those Hibs supporters who could manage to blank the semi-final capitulation to Aberdeen from their mind had a lot to be happy about. Their team had played fast, flowing, exciting football in the Hibernian way. They had played well and achieved some good results against the Old Firm and beaten Hearts convincingly twice. There were players who could score goals. Miller, Paatelainen and Latapy had all achieved double figures and Sauzée and McGinlay had chipped in, too.

Hibs' final League position of sixth should have been better. Fourth place could easily have been attained if so many points hadn't been needlessly conceded to inferior teams. Inconsistency had been Hibs' curse and addressing this would be a major target for Alex McLeish in the new season.

Most encouraging of all for those of a Hibernian persuasion, though, was the knowledge that Russell Latapy and Franck Sauzée would again be wearing the green and white in the new season. The presence of these two great players in the Hibs side should ensure another campaign of entertainment and excitement. Hopefully, too, there would be something to show for the enterprise and flair that would almost certainly be on display.

Franck Sauzée had finished the season quietly. Injuries had caused him to miss some of the final games. Despite this, Franck's outstanding contribution to the 1999–2000 campaign had resulted in him being named as the Hibs Supporters' Player of the Year. He attended the presentation dinner looking magnificent in Highland dress and dedicated his award to 'the players and staff at Hibernian but most of all the fans'.

Franck loved the fans and they loved him. That love affair was to deepen further in SPL season 2000–2001.

8

STEPPING BACK TO TAKE HIBS FORWARD

THE FOUR successive away defeats that had closed Hibs' 1999–2000 league campaign had made an impact on Alex McLeish. The manager was determined to use the close season to carry out some major surgery on his first-team squad. It is fair to say that he did not mess around.

John Hughes, Pat McGinlay, Paul Lovering and Michael Renwick were all released. They all joined Ayr United. Oli Gotskalksson was allowed to move to Brentford and Paul Hartley, about whom McLeish had never been fully convinced, was sold to St Johnstone. Kenny Miller, who had made such a huge impression the previous season, had also been transferred. His move to Rangers was received by the Hibs support with much less equanimity than the transfers of his colleagues. Hibs had received good money for Miller, but he was clearly destined for big things and most fans had hoped that the club would have held on to him for at least one more season.

There were incomings to balance the departures, though. Veteran goalkeeper Ian Westwater came in from Dunfermline to act as back-up to Nick Colgan, as well as taking on the role of goalkeeping coach. The industrious and highly skilled John O'Neil arrived from St Johnstone to boost McLeish's midfield options, and two tall defenders were added to Hibs' pool. Paul Fenwick had been around the lower divisions in Scotland for some time. He was a Canadian international and looked capable of making the step up to the SPL. Danish left back Ulrik Laursen was to prove an outstanding capture.

McLeish didn't finish his shopping spree there. He had also brought in his former Aberdeen team mate Gary Smith and Raith Rovers striker Didier Agathe on short-term deals. Smith had returned to Pittodrie after a spell in France with Rennes but hadn't been able to recapture the form he had showed in his first spell with the Dons. Agathe had goals in him and he brought pace and trickery, too.

There were two other significant moves in the summer of 2000. A sixteen-year-old local lad called Steven Whittaker was added to the ground staff and Franck Sauzée was made captain of Hibs. There was universal approval for Franck's appointment.

One of Hibs most successful skippers, all-time great Pat Stanton, had this to say, 'I was as surprised as anyone when Franck arrived at Hibs. Players of his stature are difficult to find. He may have come to Easter Road towards the twilight of his career but you simply cannot disguise his quality. Franck is a giant of a man. His presence on the park affects everyone. You can see the pride that the younger players take from playing alongside him. They look to Franck for guidance. He is a role model to them.'

Pat added, 'Franck clearly knows what the club means to Hibs supporters and to people like me. I can't think of anyone more fitting to lead our club.' Pat and Franck were similar players. Both exuded class and always seemed to have time to spare on the ball. Neither hid their commitment to the green and white jersey either.

After a pre-season tour to Germany, which saw a young striker called Tom McManus make his mark with four goals, Hibs were ready for the real stuff. Their start in the SPL was most certainly not going to be easy, as the fixture computer had directed them to Tynecastle for their first match.

Hibs fans got a shock when their team took the field. The players had agreed before the game to shave their heads as an act of team bonding. It took a second glance to recognise some of them with their newly shorn appearance. Physically imposing players like Mathias Jack and Mixu Paatelainen cut menacing figures with their recently acquired skinhead look.

Most of the hair-raising action during the match itself took place in front of the Hearts goal with Hibs, and in particular, Agathe, having the better chances to win the game. Alex McLeish had decided to change his formation. He had studied the way teams had played in the Euro 2000 tournament during the summer and had decided that most attacks were being started by a creative player at the back.

With this in mind, he switched Franck Sauzée to sweeper. Franck lined up behind two central defenders in Smith and Fenwick and played superbly. He strolled through the game, making tackles and interceptions and pinging trademark fifty-yard passes right and left with what seemed like the minimum of effort.

Playing three men in the middle of his defence allowed Alex McLeish to provide his team with added width. He introduced a wing back system. While Jack and O'Neil controlled the centre of the field, allowing Russell Latapy to link with Paatelainen and Agathe up front to cause Hearts all sorts of problems, the two wing backs used their freedom to race forward and join the attack at every opportunity. Although the game ended goalless, Hibs had posed a potent attacking threat at a ground that was notoriously difficult for visiting teams. They wasted no time in building on this encouraging start to win their next five league games in a row.

The two Dundee clubs were played off the park at Easter Road. United were beaten 3–0 with Agathe making up for his profligacy at Tynecastle with two fine goals, the second of which was a header from a swerving Sauzée free kick. Young McManus, on as a sub and looking highly promising at this stage of his career, added a third with an accomplished one-on-one finish. Most fans thought that Didier Agathe had already shown enough ability to be given a long-term contract with Hibs. Alex McLeish didn't yet feel ready to commit himself.

Agathe was on the mark again when the other Tayside team came to town. Dundee had appointed the Italian Ivano Bonetti as manager and were investing heavily, and it was to prove recklessly, in expensive foreign talent. This did them little good when they met the new Hibs. They lost five goals and two players. Fabián Caballero and Patrizio Billio were shown the red card in the forty-fifth and eighty-ninth minutes respectively and Hibs had a field day. Agathe again notched a double. One of his goals truly was a wonder strike as he beat five players before shooting home. Substitutes Dirk Lehmann (2) and Stuart Lovell were also on target in a 5–1 rout.

Sitting in the stand at the Dundee match was the recently appointed Celtic manager Martin O'Neill. He liked what he saw of Agathe and knew that he was on a three-month contract that would end soon. As soon as Agathe learned of O'Neill's interest in taking him to Parkhead, the chances of him extending his stay at Easter Road became minimal. A £50,000 transfer fee was quickly agreed and the French flyer was on his way to Celtic. O'Neill converted Agathe into a marauding wing back and it very quickly became apparent that he had made a real bargain signing. Hibs, on the other hand, had lost a potentially explosive striker.

These were exciting times at Easter Road. Franck Sauzée's best friend in football was the striker David Zitelli. They had played together at both club and under-21 international level. Zitelli was now available and Franck brought this to the attention of his boss.

Zitelli had been at Hibs' First Division Championship celebration match against Falkirk at the end of the previous season as a guest of Franck. He had liked what he had seen and it wasn't difficult to persuade him to join up with his old pal at Easter Road. With a record of eighty-three goals in 297 league games in France, there was no doubt whatsoever about Zitelli's pedigree. His recruitment ensured that the disappointment attached to the loss of Agathe was shortlived.

Also on the goal trail were teenagers Garry O'Connor and Derek Riordan. They had both scored in a pre-season friendly match against Craigroyston and Riordan revealed after the match that he had been the top scorer in every school and boys' club team he had played for. He clearly had his sights set on replicating that success at Easter Road. Another man proclaiming his goal-scoring prowess was John O'Neil. O'Neil hadn't yet scored for Hibs, but he reminded everyone that he had scored for Dundee United in a Scottish Cup Final and notched his first goal for St Johnstone against none other than Peter Schmeichel in a tour game against Brondby.

Russell Latapy had made a superb start to the season and he, too, was attracting praise. Goal-scoring machine Lawrie Reilly had this to say about Latapy: 'What a super player he is. He reminds me of Bobby Johnstone in our Famous Five forward line.'

Proof that disappointment from Hibs' anti-climactic finish to the previous season still lingered was seen in the attendance at the match against Dundee United. It was only 9,541. However, there was clear evidence that the fans were getting their belief back when 12,705 turned up for the following match against Dundee.

When Kilmarnock and Aberdeen were seen off in successive away games, Hibs found themselves at the top of the league. Paatelainen scored in both games and celebrated with a somersault. No one realised then that this trademark celebration would be witnessed three times on one ultra special evening in less than two months' time.

Hibs' new system was working well with Sauzée continually breaking from the back. When he did this, Mathias Jack filled in the gap he had left behind. Next to fall prey to the rampant Hibees were St Mirren, who were beaten 2–0 at Easter Road thanks to two goals from Stuart Lovell. Lovell was now playing as a nominal right back but this had in no way curbed his attacking instincts. Both his goals were laid on by sweeper supreme Sauzée. The second came from a magnificent cross-field pass.

Lovell has no doubts as to why he was converted into a wing back. 'Alex McLeish wanted thinking players who could bomb forward but get back and defend when a move broke down. The three players at the club with most stamina were Mixu Paatelainen,

Ulrik Laursen and myself. Mixu, despite his size, could run all day and Ulrik and I had good engines, too. I wasn't at all surprised when the boss asked Ulrik and me to be the wing backs in his new formation.

'We had played a diamond the previous season and had definitely lacked width. Franck going back to sweeper was a natural progression for him at that stage of his career and it was an easy position for such a great player. He read the game so well and would stride out past the opposing strikers with ease and start attacks for us.'

Hibs now travelled to Parkhead to put their title-seeking credentials to the stiffest of tests. Martin O'Neill had inherited players such as Lubo Moravcik, Paul Lambert, Johann Mjällby, Alan Stubbs and Henrik Larsson. He had spent extravagantly to add Chris Sutton, Alan Thompson and Joos Valgaeren to his squad, with John Hartson and Neil Lennon to follow. There was also the recently acquired Didier Agathe to reckon with.

The game in front of a highly partisan 60,000 crowd was evenly contested until John Rowbotham, the referee, awarded Celtic a controversial penalty. As Sauzée and Thompson chased a bouncing ball back towards Hibs' goal, the midfielder appeared to pull Franck out of the way. Rowbotham did not blow his whistle but he did seconds later. Nick Colgan had come out of his goal to punch the loose ball clear. He made clear contact with the ball but caught Thompson in his follow through. Rowbotham immediately pointed to the spot.

Larsson scored and Celtic went on to win 3–0. Hibs didn't go down without a fight as Jonathan Gould in the Celtic goal made a great save from a stinging Sauzée shot and Mixu Paatelainen had a strong penalty appeal turned down.

Russell Latapy had been quiet at Parkhead (he often was) but he was back to his best when Hibs beat Falkirk at Brockville in the League Cup. Latapy had been given a night off by his manager but when Hibs trailed 1–0 as the game neared completion, the little man from Trinidad was asked to come off the bench and work some of his magic. He did exactly that with two superbly taken late goals to see Hibs through to the next round. Sauzée, in this match, was described as being in 'imperious form at the heart of the Hibs defence'.

Another popular player now left Easter Road as Shaun Dennis was allowed to return to Raith Rovers. Hibs returned to their winning ways in the league with a 2–0 home win over Motherwell. Big Paatelainen, who was on top goal-scoring form (a sign of things to come), got both goals.

The match programmes for Hibs' home games carried a feature on the team's mascot for that day. Each of the youngsters was asked to name his or her favourite player. The mascot in the programme for the Motherwell game followed in the footsteps of his counterparts for all other home games to date by nominating Franck Sauzée. This unanimous approval was a sign of both Sauzée's popularity and his majestic early season form.

Another Hibs great, the feisty little playmaker from Fife, Alex Edwards, was sounding a cautionary note in the same programme. He stated, 'It worries me how Hibs will cope when Sauzée and Latapy retire.'

No one else was looking that far ahead or harbouring such negative thoughts, though. When Hibs drew 1–1 with Dunfermline at East End Park, *The Scotsman* described Sauzée's performance thus – 'Once again the Hibs captain Franck Sauzée strolled through the game, making a decisive interception here and an incisive pass there.'

It got even better at McDiarmid Park when Hibs beat St Johnstone 3–0 with goals from Sauzée, Latapy and (his first for the club) Zitelli. Franck's goal was a 'marvellous strike from a free kick', Russell was on target after a trademark dribble and shot, and Zitelli scored 'a wonderful goal from a wonderful Latapy pass'.

In-form Mixu Paatelainen praised his skipper. He said, 'Franck has given us a lot of confidence this season. He lifts everyone around him.' Not forgetting little Latapy, he added, 'Russell, too, is a very sharp player.'

Sauzée himself had complimentary words for his friend and compatriot Zitelli. He stated, 'David Zitelli is very astute and strong and today we saw the benefits he will bring to Hibs.' BBC Radio Scotland pundit Gordon Smith also spoke out in praise of Hibs and, in truth, the compliments that were coming the club's way were fully justified. Alex McLeish's 5–3–2 system was working really well and the team, inspired by its twin talismans who were being aided and abetted by all their team mates, was playing exciting, entertaining football.

There was one very happy Hibs fan in Perth that day. The supporter who posts under the screen name 'Gala Foxes' on the Hibs.net website left the game much wealthier than he had been before kick-off, as he explains: 'I put £1 on Hibs to win 3–0 and Franck to score the first goal. I got odds of 275–1. Russell Latapy got brought down in the penalty area but the referee gave a free kick outside the box. Franck smashed it in. Of course, if it had been a penalty, Russell would have taken it and scored and my bet would have been dead in the water. With Hibs 3–0 up and a few minutes to go, Latapy scored a perfectly good fourth goal. The ref chalked it off for offside. I was the only Hibs fan cheering. When I collected my winnings, I held on to my betting slip. Later on, I got Franck to sign it and I have kept it to this day.'

Hibs sat second in the league with twenty-three points from ten games and had every reason to anticipate the forthcoming visits of Rangers and Hearts with no little confidence. At other times, such anticipation would have inevitably led to disappointment and anti-climax. This time was to be different.

9

SIX OF THE BEST

RANGERS' MULTI-MILLION-POUND squad came to Easter Road expecting a hard game. In the event, they got a bit more than that. They were outplayed by Hibs and the 1–0 defeat that they suffered probably flattered them.

Hibs' dominance began at the back and carried on through the midfield area to a highly dangerous front two. Alex McLeish's new formation was continuing to prove a real success and was perfectly suiting the talents of the players he was deploying to make it so effective.

Nick Colgan was steady in goal. The two wing backs, Stuart Lovell and Ulrik Laursen, were defending well and taking every opportunity to join the attack. Gary Smith and Paul Fenwick in central defence had been solid back four players throughout their career. Now they were proving to be a bit more than that. They were more confident on the ball and they were passing it rather than simply clearing it.

The reason for this was the influence of Franck Sauzée. Franck had played sweeper before for all of his French club sides and for the French national team. He had never played there as regularly as he was doing now with Hibs though. With his huge experience and football intelligence, the position was made for him and he was perfect for it.

Franck sat behind Smith and Fenwick and read the game. He

made tackles and interceptions and strode forward into midfield. Sometimes, he would carry the ball so far, then release an excellent pass. Other times, he would keep coming and link up with his midfield or attack. He was making Hibs more composed and more creative and, all the time he was doing this, he was coaxing, cajoling and coaching his team mates to believe in themselves and do the right things.

When Franck ventured forward, Mathias Jack slipped seamlessly back into defence to plug any gaps which had been left. Big Matty had taken to his midfield holding role with complete assurance. It was as if he had never been a centre half. He provided a protective screen in front of the back line, made and won tackles, and displayed skill that was surprising in such a big man. He would win himself time and space with some neat footwork, then move the ball on to John O'Neil or Russell Latapy. He never tried anything too ambitious but did the simple things brilliantly. O'Neil or Latapy would make incisive passes or run at defenders and cause them all sorts of problems.

Up front, big Paatelainen was in the form of his life. As much of a handful for defenders as always, Mixu was now scoring regularly and linking superbly with his new partner, David Zitelli. Franck Sauzée's best friend had taken no time to show that he wasn't just at Hibs to keep Franck company. He was an excellent player in his own right who seemed to float elegantly through games, linking the play and scoring high quality goals.

This Hibs combination decisively defeated Rangers. The only goal of the game came from Zitelli, who fastened on to an O'Neil through pass to make scoring from what looked like a difficult angle seem easy. Hibs' impressive display galvanised the crowd, who gave their team thunderous vocal support. After the match, Alex McLeish remarked, 'The noise coming down from the stands was tremendous. It was so loud that there were times when I had difficulty communicating messages to my players.'

McLeish also praised his team, 'We showed both mental strength and physical commitment today. By the end of the match, we were out on our feet.' Rangers had mounted a late rally but, marshalled by the supreme Sauzée, Hibs had stood firm. The press were unanimous in recognising the Frenchman's crucial influence. *Sunday Mail* said, 'Franck Sauzée and Paul Fenwick were magnificent at the back for Hibs,' and *The Times* added, 'Alex McLeish has pulled some shrewd tactical strokes this season, most notably moving Franck Sauzée to sweeper.'

To his credit, Rangers manager Dick Advocaat was generous in defeat. He admitted, 'In the last two years we have been lucky here, but not today.' Former Hibs striker, Keith Wright, also had something to say. Keith highlighted the contribution being made by John O'Neil when he said, 'Franck Sauzée and Russell Latapy will almost always get the praise but John O'Neil is doing brilliantly in complementing them.' O'Neil was doing so brilliantly, in fact, that Alex McLeish had allowed the talented but underachieving Grant Brebner to go to Stockport County on a three-month loan.

As the derby match with Hearts approached, then, Hibs had every reason to feel confident. They were second in the league after eleven games. They had only conceded five goals and their sole defeat had been to Celtic at Parkhead. In addition, under McLeish, they had only lost one out of five matches against their capital rivals. This was their best run of form in derbies since the beginning of the Premier League in 1975, when Hibs had remained unbeaten for the first nine games against Hearts in the new streamlined league set-up.

Looking forward to the visit of Jim Jefferies' team, Alex McLeish was cautiously optimistic. He said, 'Derby matches are always hard to predict but I know that we approach this game with confidence and we hope to make home advantage count.' Well, that confidence was to be fully justified and home advantage was made to count with a vengeance.

Since the end of World War Two, Hearts had always caused Hibs problems when the teams met. The great Easter Road team, inspired by the Famous Five, may have been the best team in Scotland but they regularly encountered difficulties when they came up against their local rivals. The Turnbull's Tornadoes outfit of the 1970s was demonstrably superior to the Hearts team of that time but, despite beating them 7–0 on their own ground as 1973 dawned, managed to lose 4–1 to them when the teams next met nine months later.

The ten-year-long Alex Miller era had been something else again on the derby front. No Hibs fan needed reminding that, under Miller, Hibs had gone twenty-two games against Hearts without a win. Followers of the Jambos, of course, took every opportunity to cast this sequence of matches up to Hibs supporters, whether they needed reminding of it or not.

So, if Hibees were taking nothing for granted as the capital match-up loomed in the autumn of the first year of the twenty-first century, it was entirely understandable. However, they need not have worried. The date of this particular Hibernian versus Heart of Midlothian fixture, Sunday, 22 October 2000, was, like Monday, 1 January 1973, destined to be etched in the mind of all Hibs supporters forever.

The Sunday evening fixture was live on Sky and most Hibs fans considered that to be a good omen as Hibs' record in live televised fixtures had been excellent since the satellite broadcaster had become involved.

As the teams took the field, there was another sign that, perhaps, something special was in the air. The end of the ground where the Hearts supporters gathered was more than half empty and the cheer which greeted the arrival of their favourites was definitely not as confident as usual. In contrast, when Hibs ran out, their fans gave them a rousing standing ovation.

Hearts started well, though. They now had former Hibs striker Gordon Durie in their ranks and a look at his former clubs was sufficient to show the quality of his pedigree. After leaving Easter Road, he had moved to Chelsea. From there he had gone on to Tottenham Hotspur before joining Rangers. Now he was a Hearts player and, in the early part of this game, despite his every touch being roundly booed by the Hibs support, he was playing a prominent part. Indeed, after only five minutes, he linked up with Steve Fulton, who set up the young Northern Irish striker Andy Kirk for the opening goal.

Only an excellent save from Nick Colgan prevented Hibs from going two down but soon the tide began to turn. A fine Russell Latapy pass created an opening for Mixu Paatelainen and only a top save from Finnish goalkeeper Antti Niemi stopped his fellow countryman from levelling the scores. Mixu then had the ball in the net with a header but referee Hugh Dallas ruled the goal out. The force was definitely with Hibs now and they scored twice in the three minutes leading up to half time to go in at the break a goal in front rather than a goal behind. Paatelainen got the goals. They were both scored from close range and neither was a thing of beauty but that didn't matter. The game had turned round and Hibs were ahead. They just about deserved to be, too.

The second half was a rout. In fifty-one minutes, Latapy, once again teasing and tormenting Hearts, released Zitelli with a superb through pass. The striker ran on and, with admirable composure, slid the ball under Niemi. This goal changed the game totally. Hearts seemed to lose hope. Hibs grew in belief. It was obvious that players like Sauzée, Latapy and Zitelli were thinking to themselves, 'We have nothing to worry about here. We have played against much better teams than this and won. We are capable of going on to a special victory here.'

That is exactly what they and their team mates proceeded to do. They exuded class and cheek and displayed a range of impudent flicks and feints that sent out a message of superiority to Hearts. The best words to describe Hibs' play come from the French heritage of Sauzée and Zitelli themselves. Hibs were elegant, nonchalant and insouciant.

The goals continued to come. Latapy passed to O'Neil who laid the ball into the pass of Paateleinen. Big Mixu crashed the ball into the net. He celebrated with a trademark somersault and then did a little dance with his captain. The French sweeper and the Finnish centre forward did what could only be described as a Highland jig of joy in front of their adoring fans. Mixu's hat trick was the first in a derby by a Hibs player since Pat Quinn had performed the feat more than thirty years previously. After his threesome, Quinn had said, 'If I had known how popular it was going to make me, I would have done it years ago.' Paatelainen, for his part, was now assured of Hibernian immortality.

Next on the scoresheet was John O'Neil, who had played brilliantly. O'Neil had worked tirelessly and used his craft to get the ball to Sauzée, Latapy and Zitelli as often as possible. Now he got the goal he deserved, crashing a Zitelli corner high into the Hearts net.

Franck Sauzée lifted O'Neil onto his shoulders in a fireman's lift and carried him across to the Hibs support to take their acclaim. Once again, Sauzée's rapport with his club's followers was instinctive and perfectly judged. This was to become an iconic image. In the days following the match, Hibs produced t-shirts with this evocative celebration emblazoned on the front. They sold very well indeed.

Hibs' last goal was the best of the lot as the majestic Latapy finished a sweeping move by volleying an unstoppable shot past Niemi. Hibs switched off in the last minute and allowed Colin Cameron to snatch a second goal for Hearts. No one seemed particularly upset. In fact, the Hibs fans rubbed salt in their rivals' wounds by greeting the goal with a mocking round of applause.

So, a historic Hibernian derby performance and victory finished with a score of 6-2. The pre-match portents of something out of the ordinary in the air had come to pass and a match to be treasured by all Hibs supporters had taken place.

There was no shortage of post-match comment. Jim Jefferies, who had once more been on the receiving end of some capital punishment was honest and direct when he said, 'This is my most disappointing night as a manager. The scoreline didn't flatter Hibs in any way.'

Alex McLeish called Hibs' win 'a vintage performance' and stated, 'It's always nice to beat your city rivals but to do it in such style was a wonderful bonus.' Former captain John Hughes chipped in with, 'Big Franck is a revelation at the back. Alex McLeish has found a magic formula.'

Hat-trick hero Mixu Paatelainen was rightly on a major high. 'It's beyond belief. You dream about nights like this,' was Mixu's take on the evening. Hibs fans felt exactly the same. This victory had indeed been a dream come true. There had been important landmarks, too. When O'Neil scored Hibs' fifth goal, it was the club's 1,000th in Premier League football. Paatelainen's third goal had been the ninety-ninth league goal of his career. If Hugh Dallas hadn't chalked off his first half header, he would have already achieved his century.

John O'Neil was delighted with his goal and with his overall performance. 'It was great to play well and score in such an important Hibs win,' he said. 'The ball landed at my feet from the corner and I could have hit it first time. I took a touch, though, and hammered it. What a feeling when it flew into the roof of the net. People should remember that Hearts were a good team at that time and it wasn't just the margin of our win, it was the manner of it. We played them off the park and they were shell shocked by the end of the game.

'It was my wife's birthday and she watched the match from the stand with two of our friends. We had planned to go out afterwards but it would have been a quiet night if Hearts had won. In the event, we had a great celebration.'

Hibs' two top men had their say as well. Latapy, who seemed to treat Hearts as his personal plaything, a team to tantalise, torture and terminate, was first to offer his opinion. 'Hibs fans want flair and Franck and I supplied it,' he said. This may not have been modest but it was perfectly true.

The last word went to Sauzée himself. He stated, 'The team is now playing 100% with its mind and there is confidence in our passing. That is what I wanted Hibernian to achieve. When we beat Hearts 6–2, every player wanted to put his foot on the ball. That was fantastic football.'

There was more to come. Franck paid tribute to his big friend Paatelainen. He said, 'Mixu is an important player for us. He is a big character on the pitch and in the dressing room.' The Gallic Great next produced words that were music to Hibs fans' ears: 'Hibernian are now a name again,' he declared. 'Every team wants to beat us.'

Sauzée showed just how happy he was when he compared the atmosphere in the Hibs dressing room to that he had experienced when winning the European Cup with Marseille. He spoke of being stopped in the street by fans and congratulated after the Hearts game. He said, 'Knowing your supporters love you makes you feel good. When you feel good, you perform on the pitch.' He finished with, 'If it hadn't been for Niemi, the score against Hearts might have been 8–2 or 9–2.'

Most Hibs supporters were more than happy with 6–2. It had been a magical night but it was now time to move on. The big challenge for Alex McLeish and his talented team was to carry their current, irresistible form into the remainder of the season. McLeish did allow his team a little celebration of their landmark victory, though. When the players reported for training the day after the game, a few bottles of champagne were opened in the dressing room. Each player had one paper cup of bubbly and then got on with training as usual!

As well as a fine team, Hibs now also had strength in depth. This was demonstrated by the fact that players as good as Grant Brebner, Derek Collins, Martin McIntosh, Tom McManus, Ian Murray and Tom Smith were unable to command a regular place in the team.

Indeed, against Hearts, a player as vital as Matty Jack had broken his toe and gone off, yet had hardly been missed. Jack's replacement, Lyndon Andrews, yet another McLeish signing, this time from Russell Latapy's homeland of Trinidad and Tobago, had come on to play a part in Hibernian history.

It was time for Hibs to get their feet back on the ground, though, and the next match would ensure that happened. Just six days after demolishing Hearts, Hibs headed to Tannadice for a meeting with Dundee United.

Most of their followers, if they were completely honest with themselves, would have admitted that they expected a come down from the previous week's high. Life as a Hibee has always been a roller-coaster ride and consistency has never been high on the list of attributes associated with Hibernian Football Club.

There was to be no anti-climax this time, though. Hibs fans travelled North in large numbers and were rewarded with a 1–0 win courtesy of a late Tom McManus goal. The young striker, hailed as an outstanding prospect at that time, came off the bench to win the game with an eighty-first minute shot. The highlight of the afternoon for most was the celebrating of the captain's birthday. Franck Sauzée was thirty-five years young on the day of the match and his adoring public serenaded him with renditions of 'Happy Birthday to You' throughout the match. At full time, Franck went to the crowd to acknowledge their good wishes. The cheer he received was almost as loud as the roar that had greeted McManus' goal a few minutes earlier. It has to be said that there was no sign of age diluting Sauzée's powers, as the big man had strolled the game in his usual imperious fashion.

Then came the anticipated blip. Hibs lost 2–1 in the League Cup at Rugby Park to a Kilmarnock side that was going particularly well at that time. Russell Latapy scored an outstanding opening goal, leaving two defenders and the goalkeeper on their back before stroking the ball casually into the empty net, but Kilmarnock came back to win with the deciding goal being scored, ironically, by Craig Dargo.

Dargo was, and is, a Hibs supporter. He had trained at Easter Road as a youngster but was never offered a full-time contract with the club he loved. Over the years, in the colours of a variety of teams, he has been a thorn in Hibs' flesh. He was exactly that as, on a cold Ayrshire night, Hibs exited a competition that they had a great chance of winning.

Franck Sauzée and David Zitelli both missed this match through injury and their absence was keenly felt. They were back the following weekend, though, when the Hibs show got well and truly back on the road. Dens Park was the venue and the match was in Hibs' favourite Sunday night Sky Television slot.

A 3–1 win was no less than the Hibees deserved. Zitelli got two goals and the second was a Wayne Rooney style bicycle kick, which had to be an early contender for goal of the season.

The French striker now had four goals in four starts and was clearly an accomplished finisher. His in-swinging corners were also major weapons that caused defences all sorts of problems. Hearts had failed to deal with them in the recent derby and it wasn't difficult to see why as the left-footed Zitelli homed the ball in on goal from the right corner flag with power and pace.

A chance for revenge followed when Kilmarnock visited Easter Road on league duty. A crowd of 12,588 turned out, which showed that the team had caught the interest of its support.

Hibs played well and Paatelainen duly scored his 100th league goal, which he had so nearly recorded in the derby. However, Sauzée had to go off with a recurrence of his injury and Paul Wright, another Killie striker with Hibs connections, pulled his team level. The draw was a disappointment but the result had to be placed in the context of Kilmarnock's position in the league – they were fourth, one point ahead of Rangers – and the enforced loss of Sauzée.

Asked after the game who were the best players he had played with and against in his lengthy career with Dundee United, Aberdeen, Bolton, Wolves and Hibs, Big Mixu answered unhesitatingly: 'Franck Sauzée and Russell Latapy are very high on my list.'

Sauzée may have been unable to play but he was available for interview. He confirmed his continuing happiness at Easter Road and declared, 'I am proud to be captain of Hibs. It is a great honour.' The Hibs faithful revered Franck as a player but they also loved him as a man. His devotion to Hibs was obvious and sincere and that put the great man on a pedestal in the eyes of his supporters. Franck also revealed how much he was enjoying playing sweeper. He said that he was running far less than he had been doing in midfield and was no longer over tired after games.

Franck attempted a comeback in the next match against Aberdeen but had to go off again, as did Ulrik Laursen. The young Ian Murray came on but wasn't able to help his team mates prevent a disappointing defeat. It was surely no coincidence that in almost all the games that Hibs had lost or drawn, Sauzée had been absent through injury for all or part of the match.

Franck was still missing in Hibs' next game at Paisley, and a wrongly disallowed Paatelainen goal and a last minute St Mirren equaliser cancelled out John O'Neil's early strike to leave Hibs with another disappointing draw.

To the delight of the Hibs support, Sauzée was back for the visit of league leaders Celtic. Martin O'Neill's men were flying but Hibs brought them back down to earth. An excellent game finished goalless and Hibs' skipper played the highly rated Henrik Larsson out of the game. Another outstanding home performer was Matty Jack. The big man's superb midfield display earned him the accolade in the press of being 'one of the best players in the league this season'.

Next up was another Sunday evening Sky special at Fir Park, Motherwell. A 3–1 victory in no way flattered Hibs and Zitelli was at it again. Derek Townsley, soon to be a Hibs player, provided an own goal and the French ace got the other two. His second goal was a stunning rocket shot struck with astounding velocity.

Once again, the tributes were flying in the media. On Radio Scotland, the venerable Bob Crampsey spoke glowingly about Zitelli's wonder strike. He said, 'You won't see a better goal this season.' That is exactly what the experts had been saying about DZ's goal at Dundee a few weeks earlier.

On the same channel, Chick Young had this to say: 'Hibs are a team I would pay money to go and watch. The way they pass the ball is wonderful and their flair players are excellent.'

A star in the great Marseille team which won the Champions' League. Illustrious team mates include Fabien Barthez, Rudi Voller, Marcel Desailly, Alen Boksic and Didier Deschamps.

© SNS GROUP

A championship-clinching goal. Franck puts Hibs ahead against Falkirk at Easter Road on the day the 1998-99 First Division Championship trophy was presented and he celebrates in style with the help of Mixu Paatelainen.

© SNS GROUP

Franck drives home a typical thunderbolt shot against Hearts in the Millennium Derby at Tynecastle. The celebration which followed is almost as famous as the goal itself.

Franck is SPL Player of the Month for March 2000 after scoring a goal against Hearts which cost him four of his front teeth. The dental repair work has clearly been successful.

A man with a passion for Hibernian. Franck shows just how much it means to score for his beloved Hibees. Paul Fenwick and Tom McManus look on.

A Sauzee free kick special against St Johnstone in September 2000. This goal helped one Hibs supporter to win a 275-1 bet.

Joy unconfined as Franck and Mixu celebrate after the 6-2 derby demolition. The hat trick hero is making sure that he hangs on to the match ball.

The French connection. Franck and David Zitelli take delivery of a new set of wheels.

The old main stand has been demolished and Franck leads Hibs out to face St Mirren through the debris of that famous structure. As he does so, the club plays La Marseillaise, a gesture which meant a lot to the Hibs skipper.

Hibs have just beaten Livingston to reach the 2001 Scottish Cup final and Franck shows the fans just how pleased he is.

Franck tries the Scottish Cup for size in the lead-up to the 2001 final against Celtic.

Captain Sauzee and Hibs' two mascots on Scottish Cup Final Day. It has to be said that none of them looks particularly confident.

Spot on! Franck scores a penalty against Motherwell in one of his final games for Hibs.

A Scottish Cup dream destroyed. Franck lies devastated on the Hampden turf after Celtic beat Hibs 3-0 in the 2001 final.

Shedding blood for the cause. Franck has to leave the field after cutting his eye against AEK Athens in the UEFA Cup.

Manager of Hibs. Franck attempts to get to grips with the switch from the playing field to the technical area.

The saddest of farewells. Franck leaves Easter Road after losing his job as manager. The fans, faithful to the last, applaud him on his way. Franck's disappointment is written all over his face.

A true Hibs legend in one of his most famous moments.

SAUZÉE
"LE GOD"

Still an icon after all these years – gone but not forgotten. A banner commemorating Le God
is unfolded at Easter Road in 2011.

Both flair players were at the top of their games. Sauzée was fully fit again, commanding defensively and creative going forward. Latapy was at his best in Hibs' next match, a 3–0 home win over Dunfermline. He brilliantly laid on goals for Paatelainen and Zitelli and drew this praise from former Hibs great Peter Cormack: 'Russell is a hot property. His first touch is superb and he has the ability to see things that others can't. Russell is the playmaker and he will make things happen.'

Trinidad and Tobago manager Ian Porterfield had attended the Dunfermline game and described Latapy simply as 'a wee genius'. The big genius, meanwhile, was also making his presence felt. Sauzée's return had seen Hibs get back to winning ways and this continued with the visit of St Johnstone. A 'peach of a goal' from the underrated Stuart Lovell and another from Big Mixu, his tenth of the season, comfortably saw off the Perth men.

Hibs' last match before Christmas was a trip to Ibrox. There was a huge Hibs support and they saw their team play well but lose 1–0. A contributory factor in the defeat was the harsh sending off of John O'Neil.

There was no time for the Easter Road men to feel sorry for themselves, though. Boxing Day brought a visit to Tynecastle and a confrontation with a Hearts team thirsting for revenge after its recent 6–2 thrashing. The game ended 1–1 but Hibs could easily have won convincingly. Latapy again gave Hearts a torrid time, Lovell scored what was described as a 'Lovelly' goal and Hibs passed up a host of chances. Lovell's goal was so good that he received a compliment from Hearts goalkeeper Antti Niemi at full time. The Finn remarked on the swift incisive passing that had set the chance up for the wing back. He then highlighted the speed with which Lovell had hit his first-time side-foot shot. 'The strike was so instantaneous,' he said, 'that I had no time to react.'

The post-match quotes summed up Hibs' domination. New Hearts manager Craig Levein, (Jim Jefferies had gone to Bradford), showed he was comfortable with a cliché when he said, 'There were times when Hibs carved through our defence like a knife through butter.' He added, 'Antti Niemi pulled off some great saves.'

Alex McLeish agreed with his rival's assessment. He declared, 'We played some lovely football against a team very fired up for the occasion. It is a measure of how far the club's expectations have come when people are disappointed with a draw at Tynecastle.' That was perfectly true and Matty Jack had the last word on the Christmas derby when, with an interesting turn of phrase, he passed the opinion that, 'Hibs are flying with wings and playing marvellous football.'

This marvellous football had led to an accolade for the team's two main men. The BBC's *Match of the Day* programme's Scottish players of the season list showed Russell Latapy and Franck Sauzée in first and second place with 1,034 and 1,033 points respectively.

The hectic festive season schedule continued with two more home matches for Hibs against the Dundee teams. The first game against Dundee United ended in controversy and a win. In the final minute of the game, Dundee United kicked the ball out of play. They expected Matty Jack to return the ball to them but instead he launched a long throw into the penalty area. The ball was cleared for a corner but when the flag kick came over, referee Alan Freeland, never a man for remaining inconspicuous, awarded a penalty kick as he adjudged that Craig Easton had fouled Jack. This enraged the Tannadice men and after Latapy had coolly converted the spot kick to seal victory, mayhem broke out.

On the final whistle, United's Hibs-supporting goalie Alan Combe was shown a red card for overdoing his protests and the Tayside staff and players surrounded the officials. Mr Freeland, though, had made his decision and he was sticking to it. Hibs were just happy to bank another three points.

They collected three more on 2 January 2001 against Dundee with an easy 3–0 win. This was the last game before the winter break and Scottish football would not resume until 27 January, when Hibs would meet Clyde in the Scottish Cup. As soon as the Dundee match was over, work was to begin on demolishing the old centre stand, with the intention of having an impressive new West Stand in its place in time for the start of season 2001–2002.

The year 2000 had marked the 125th anniversary of Hibs' formation. The club ended it by holding a competition that challenged supporters to predict what would be happening at Easter Road in 2125, 125 years further on. The value Hibs fans attached to their skipper was demonstrated by one Hibee's entry. He expressed the wish that in 2125, Franck Sauzée would be about to put pen to paper and sign his latest one-year contract extension!

Alex McLeish may have been harbouring similar thoughts as he praised his captain. He said, 'Franck Sauzée, at thirty-five years old, has produced four top performances in eight days.' These performances had helped Hibs reach second place in the SPL. They had fifty-four points from twenty-five matches and had only lost three games in the league.

As Sauzée and his team mates eyed the prospect of the winter break, their club's supporters wondered whether the team's interminable wait for Scottish Cup glory, which now stretched to ninety-nine years, might end before 2125. The more optimistic among them allowed themselves the luxury of considering the possibility that 2001 might indeed be Hibs' year.

10

CUP FINAL CAPTAIN

HIBS RETURNED to action in late January 2001 with twin objectives. They wanted to retain their current third spot in the SPL until the end of the season and, more than that, much more than that, they wanted to lift the Scottish Cup.

Their first task in the national cup competition was to beat First Division Clyde. This they accomplished with ease. Clyde were disposed of by six goals to one. Dirk Lehmann and Grant Brebner were back in Hibs' starting line-up with Brebner fresh from his recently concluded loan spell with Stockport County.

Both played well. Indeed, Lehmann notched two goals. Ulrik Laursen, Mathias Jack, Mixu Paatelainen and captain Sauzée were also on target. Franck's goal was a free kick that crashed in off the cross bar. The *Evening News* called his shot 'stunning'. His hairstyle was pretty eye catching, too, as the skipper had used some of his mid-season break time to have his locks dyed blond.

As soon as the sixth goal went in, the Hibs fans begun to indulge in one of their favourite chants. Three months earlier, they had shouted, 'We want seven,' in the 6–2 derby defeat of Hearts. Now they repeated their call as their favourites looked to add further goals against Clyde. Once again, a seventh goal proved elusive and a certain New Year's Day score line from 1973 was able to maintain its uniqueness.

Older Hibs supporters would have recalled that it had been Clyde, then a top team in the top league, who had defeated Hibs in the 1958 Scottish Cup Final. This had happened after Hibs had beaten Hearts and Rangers on their way to the final. Since then, the sides had met four times in the cup and Hibs had won on every occasion. Most Hibs fans would gladly have swapped all four of these victories, though, to have lifted the trophy at Hampden in 1958.

However, there had been no problems this time. As one Sunday newspaper put it, 'Hibs progressed without pain or pressure.' Alex McLeish was tuned in to his club's supporters' wavelength when he said, 'The Scottish Cup remains a competition which has haunted Hibs fans for decades. We would dearly love to get our hands on the trophy.' Celtic's European Cup-winning captain Billy McNeill was of the opinion that this could be Hibs' year. He also added, 'Alex McLeish has done a superb job at Hibs.'

McLeish had done a superb job and was continuing to do so. Hibs resumed league duty with a visit to Kilmarnock. These two teams had fought out closely contested matches all season and this latest encounter was no exception. Hibs were grateful for a late Ulrik Laursen equaliser and the big Dane had now scored three goals in quick succession. Commenting on his sudden, prolific scoring streak, Laursen said, 'I usually only score one goal per year so that will be me for the next three years!'

When Hibs ran out to face St Mirren in their next match, the old main stand had been demolished and that side of the ground resembled a building site. There was joy in the air as Franck Sauzée had just signed another new contract. This one was due to keep him at Easter Road until the summer of 2003, when he would be approaching his thirty-eighth birthday. To mark the occasion, 'Le Marseillaise' was played over the public address system as Franck led his team onto the field.

It was clear that Sauzée was very moved by this gesture and he started the game in great style. After smashing in another of his trademark free kicks to put Hibs ahead, Franck ran to the old East

Terracing part of the ground, stood to attention and saluted the fans. It was a special moment.

Approaching the hour mark in the match, though, Hibs found themselves trailing 2–1. At that point, they changed gear and rattled in three quick goals to ease their supporters' worries. David Zitelli scored twice and Russell Latapy added the other after a twinkle-toed dribble and a sublime finish. If Sauzée specialised in rocket free kicks, then Latapy went in for his own brand of solo efforts.

The Herald noted Hibs' new-found capacity for fighting back and reminded readers of Franck Sauzée's 'long held doctrine that the sign of a good team is how they perform in troubled times'. Hibs also had to show fortitude when they visited Forthbank to play Stirling in the next round of the Scottish Cup. Albion took the lead in only four minutes with a Chris Templeman wonder strike that had 'cup-tie upset goal' written all over it.

Fortunately, Franck Sauzée yet again found the net. He was thirty-five years old and playing in defence, but he couldn't stop scoring. John O'Neil added another goal and the normal order seemed to have been restored. However, Stirling just would not lie down. They found an equaliser and, with former Hibs goalkeeper Chris Reid in inspired form between their posts, pushed Hibs all the way. Fortunately for Hibs and their worried fans, in a ground that, by then, was enshrouded in mist, substitute Tom McManus popped up with a late winning goal to send the greens into the quarter finals.

Hibs returned to their Sunday night Sky Television slot to face Martin O'Neill's all-conquering Celtic side at Parkhead and came away with an impressively earned 1–1 draw. Another new Alex McLeish signing, Frenchman Marc Libbra, scored Hibs' goal after linking with David Zitelli. To complete the French connection, Libbra had played with Franck Sauzée at Marseille earlier in his career. Sauzée himself was in prime form at Celtic Park. After one particularly composed and cultured piece of play, he received an ovation from the Celtic faithful – a rare accolade indeed.

Then came evidence of the fickleness of football. Tom Smith, who had started the season as a first team regular and who was still in his twenties, was forced to retire. Smith had been unfortunate with injuries throughout his career and had been injured again back in November in the match against Aberdeen. Now the doctors had told him that the knee problem he had sustained against the Dons was of a degenerative nature. If Smith continued playing, he faced the prospect of permanent disability. He had no option but to hang up his boots. While the rest of the Hibs squad anticipated a possible cup final appearance later in the season, poor Smith could only contemplate a life without football and the prospect of finding alternative employment.

The quarter final draw for the Scottish Cup sent Hibs to Rugby Park for their fifth meeting of the season with Bobby Williamson's Kilmarnock. All the previous matches between the teams had been closely contested and this was no exception. Hibs lost their inspirational skipper in the first half and their dream of finally annexing Scottish football's oldest trophy seemed to be in real danger until Tom McManus again made a crucial contribution. Young Tom wasn't the tallest of players but he leapt prodigiously in the eighty-first minute to meet a Russell Latapy cross at the back post and bullet a header into the net.

McManus' goal was enough to take Hibs into the semi-final for the second year in a row. The draw was kind to Hibs because they were paired with First Division leaders Livingston when they could easily have come up against Celtic. Maybe the prospect of the forthcoming semi-final match proved a distraction for Hibs, because they proceeded to draw one and lose three of their next four league games against Motherwell, Dunfermline, Aberdeen and St Johnstone.

A much more plausible reason for this sudden dip in form was the continuing absence through injury of Franck Sauzée. To that point of the season, Sauzée had played twenty-seven matches and Hibs had lost only three of them. Of the six games he had missed through injury, Hibs had drawn two and lost four. These statistics were stark and clearly demonstrated the captain's importance to the team.

Sauzée was back for the league visit of Rangers and his impact was immediate. Hibs played better and secured a goalless draw. Hibs had yet another new signing on view and he was the latest French player to join up at Easter Road. Alex McLeish had been tracking midfielder Freddy Arpinon for some time and now he had his man. There were no transfer windows back then and clubs could buy and sell players at any time, which made things much more exciting for supporters.

Mind you, Hibs' acquisition was dwarfed by Rangers' latest foray into the transfer market. Dick Advocaat had just paid Chelsea £12 million for the signature of striker Tore André Flo. This was extravagance on a grand scale. One wondered why Rangers needed another striker at all. They had signed Kenny Miller from Hibs at the start of the season but Advocaat had seemed reluctant to select Miller on a regular basis. In one of his rare starts, Miller had scored five goals in one game against St Mirren. That should have told his manager something.

Franck Sauzée had been his usual imperious self against Rangers, prompting one newspaper to state, 'Sauzée is arguably the best reader of a game in Scottish football.' As far as Hibs fans were concerned, there was no argument about it.

Another player who had impressed against the Ibrox men was Grant Brebner, who was now back to something close to his best form. This was encouraging for Hibs as they prepared for the Scottish Cup semi-final with Livingston at Hampden. The previous season's capitulation to Aberdeen at the same stage was all too fresh in every Hibee's mind and no one wanted a repeat. There was good news, too, when it was announced that Ulrik Laursen and Nick Colgan had extended their contracts, but concern arose when it was learned that, as yet, Russell Latapy hadn't agreed to put pen to paper.

Livingston, under the stewardship at that time of Dominic Keane, were well on course to win the First Division and join the

SPL. The investment of Keane and his fellow directors Willie Haughey and John McGuinness had brought players like Darren Jackson, Barry Wilson, Steven Tosh, Marvin Andrews, Michael Hart and David Fernández to Almondvale. Livingston would clearly be no pushovers.

It was important that Hibs made a good start and that is exactly what they did. Latapy laid the ball into John O'Neil's path and the little midfield dynamo dispatched a fine shot past Livingston goalkeeper Ian McCaldon. The West Lothian team fought back hard but Hibs, backed by a huge and noisy green and white bedecked support, finished the game as a contest with second half goals from Zitelli (his tenth of the season) and O'Neil once again.

O'Neil's brother Steven was being married as the semi-final took place. John should have been acting as his brother's best man. This had proved impossible, so he had compensated by being the best man on the pitch at Hampden. This consistent and talented player thoroughly deserved his Man of the Match award.

John recalls the day fondly. 'After the game, I headed off to the hotel to join my brother's wedding reception. As I walked into the hall where it was taking place, everyone started to applaud. I was really touched but didn't want to take away from my brother's big day by stealing the limelight. However, when I looked across, the man himself was leading the ovation, which was a lovely touch.'

Not far behind O'Neil in the performance stakes was Franck Sauzée. Sauzée lit up the semi-final with a moment of magic. As he and two Livingston forwards chased a through ball towards the Hibs goal, Franck casually flicked the ball over his head in the opposite direction to which all three players were running. He then turned, took control of the ball again and sent one of his trademark passes to a colleague. All the while, the Livingston attackers kept running towards the Hibs goal wondering where on earth the ball had gone. This magnificent piece of cheeky skill sent the Hibs fans into raptures.

Around 20,000 Hibs supporters had travelled through to Glasgow for the semi-final. No doubt many of them had made the same journey just a year earlier and seen their hopes dashed when Aberdeen had played above themselves and Hibs had failed to perform to their full potential. This time, things had been different. Hibs were stronger now and had dealt comfortably with a spirited and not untalented Livingston team.

Hibs hadn't been at their free flowing best but they had done enough to qualify for the final and to give their supporters hope for the outcome of that match when it came round. Hibs would face Celtic at Hampden on the last day of the season. The Glasgow giants had enjoyed a magnificent season under Martin O'Neill, who had spent big and built a physically strong, disciplined, impressive side, which also contained some very skilful players. Most of all, Celtic had hardly lost a game all season. The 'Battle of the Greens' on Saturday, 26 May, was a great opportunity for Hibs to break their Scottish Cup hoodoo at last. It also promised to be a massive challenge.

The hunger of the Hibs support to lift the cup was palpable. As *Scotland on Sunday* reported after the semi-final, 'In the end, ears were deafened by the Hibs throng. It must seem like 2,000 years to them since their club last lifted the Scottish Cup.'

It was in fact ninety-nine years and one of those who had tried but failed to win a Scottish Cup Final at Hampden for the team he loved, Pat Stanton, had encouraging words for the Hibs faithful. Pat predicted, 'This could just be our year. Hibs at their best are capable of beating anyone, so Hibs fans have every right to look forward to the final.' Stanton's advice to the players was, 'Don't be frightened of it.'

Franck Sauzée expressed similar thoughts. He said, 'Alex McLeish, Rod Petrie and I speak the same football language. This season we have been magnificent at times. The most important thing is mentality. We must have a strong mental attitude.'

David Zitelli, whose fine goal had extinguished any hopes of a Livingston revival, had this to say: 'Franck made the difference to us today. He is important to the whole team. He showed us what was necessary to win today. He took his time and was composed and, for strikers, that is important, because he delivers a good ball to us.'

The Scottish Cup may have been uppermost in everyone's minds but there was still league business to attend to. First, there was a 1–1 draw with Kilmarnock, the third share of the points between the teams in the league in the course of the season. New signing Marc Libbra scored Hibs' goal. The tall French centre forward could hold the ball up, was skilful for a big man and had an educated left foot and an eye for goal. He had been signed on loan until the end of the season but was already looking like a player Hibs would like to secure on a permanent deal.

Libbra and his French striking colleague Zitelli were again on target when Hibs beat Dundee 2–0 at Dens Park. A seventeen-year-old centre forward called Garry O'Connor came on for the last twenty minutes to make his debut in this match. This was part of a triumvirate of matches against Dundee for the big striker from Prestonpans. Just before his first team entrance, O'Connor and his strike partner, fellow seventeen-year-old Derek Riordan, had both scored as Hibs under-18s had beaten Dundee. Just after that full debut, O'Connor made the dark blues suffer again when he scored five times against them in an under-21 game.

Now came a cup final rehearsal against Celtic at Easter Road. The hoops were already SPL champions. They had lost only one league match out of thirty-five played and showed why when they beat Hibs 5–2. This was a misleading score, though. Hibs made and missed a host of chances while Celtic were clinical. At one point, Hibs had been 5–0 down before two late strikes from Libbra had put a more respectable gloss on the score line.

Alex McLeish was undaunted. He said, 'I told my players after the game that they had played well and didn't deserve to lose. I also mentioned to them the number of chances they had made and this must give them fantastic encouragement for the final.' McLeish may have been employing some effective psychology to ensure that his players did not approach the final feeling apprehensive but there was truth in his words. Hibs hadn't played badly and the score had flattered Celtic. There was still hope for the big day when it came round.

What came next was the final derby of the season against Hearts. The feature photograph for the match programme was of Russell Latapy. This was rather ironic, as Latapy would not be playing in this game. Indeed, he would never play for Hibs again.

The Little Magician's form had faded since the SPL had resumed after the winter break. He had also failed to date to renew his contract. Hibs are believed to have made him a most generous offer but Latapy had declined to accept it. Now, he blotted his copybook. The match with Hearts was scheduled for the Sunday evening Sky slot. On the Friday before the derby, Russell went out with his close friend, the Manchester United striker, Dwight Yorke. It is fair to say that they enjoyed a highly sociable evening. Unfortunately, it did not come to a positive end as Latapy was stopped by the police on suspicion of driving under the influence of alcohol.

The tabloid newspapers went to town and the build up to the derby game was overshadowed by wall-to-wall coverage of Latapy's misdemeanours. There was no way that the Trinidadian would be selected for the Hearts fixture, which was a shame because he was inevitably at his best against the men from Tynecastle. Even without their playmaker, Hibs dominated the match but, just like against Celtic the previous week, missed chances galore.

Mixu Paatelainen even missed a penalty when he tried to be clever and dink his shot over the diving Antti Niemi. The ball beat the goalkeeper but instead of hitting the back of the net, it struck the cross bar and bounced to safety. It was lost on no one that if Latapy had been playing, he would have taken the spot kick, would almost certainly have scored and Alex McLeish would have been celebrating another derby victory. In the event, the manager and the Hibs support had to settle for a 0–0 draw.

Ian Murray, who was starting to establish himself as a first team regular at this point, remembers being surprised when he returned to the dressing room after the match. 'Alex McLeish was raging at Franck Sauzée,' says Murray. He thought Franck should have taken the penalty and was telling him so in no uncertain terms. Franck didn't argue. He said, "You're right. I should have hit it." I couldn't help thinking that Mixu, who had missed the spot kick after all, was getting off pretty lightly.'

As Stuart Lovell reveals, though, Paatelainen didn't totally escape the manager's wrath. 'It was the only time I ever saw Alex McLeish angry with Franck. He wasn't best pleased with Mixu either. He thought that he had tried to be too smart against his friend and Finnish international team mate Niemi and had tried to make a point by chipping the penalty down the middle of the goal. Mixu denied this and they had a right ding dong. Mixu ended up swearing in Finnish, which was a sure sign that he was angry. The great thing about Alex as a boss, though, was that he never held any grudges. If you had something out with him, then that was that. When you came in for training next day, it was finished and forgotten.'

Murray was taken aback at Latapy's behaviour. He said, 'We were all baffled by what Russell had done. He liked a night out but he usually kept his socialising for after a match, not before it. To go out on the town before such an important game was just not like him at all.'

Hibs had one final league fixture to fulfil. They had to visit Ibrox to play Rangers and it was a game they could have done without. Latapy was again an absentee and unsurprisingly, with the Scottish Cup Final only six days away, Hibs were not at their best.

Rangers won 4–0 but that wasn't the worst of it. With time running out, Rangers had the opportunity for a fifth goal. Many players would have accepted the loss of another goal as disappointing but not crucial. Franck Sauzée felt differently. Hibs skipper was a man of immense professional pride and he launched himself into a full-stretch, goal-saving tackle. Franck's tackle did indeed prevent Rangers from scoring but he injured himself in the process. He had to be carried from the field and a wave of despair spread through both the Hibs fans in the ground and those at home listening to the game on the radio.

In the week leading up to the Cup Final, Hibs announced that Russell Latapy would not be involved at Hampden. He had, in fact, agreed to sign for Rangers.

At the time, and indeed many times since, Hibs fans – including the author of this book – have pondered whether Alex McLeish should have put pragmatism before principle and played Latapy one last time in the final. People behind the scenes at Easter Road have subsequently confirmed that this would not have been a viable option, since the player was not in the correct frame of mind at that time to have done himself or his team justice.

Nick Colgan agrees with this view. 'It would have been great to have had Russell available but you have to keep club rules. What Alex McLeish did was hard but also correct. If you allow one player to take liberties, then everyone else thinks that they can do the same.'

Stuart Lovell isn't so sure. 'Most of the players wanted Russell to play and you could see that in his own understated way he was really disappointed that he had been banished from the first team squad. It must have been a massive boost for Celtic to know that Franck was injured and that Russell wasn't going to be playing. They were our two inspirational players and I know how we would have felt if Henrik Larsson or Chris Sutton had been missing from their team.'

It was sad to see such a talented player's time at Hibs fizzle out in anti-climax. Russell Latapy was a highly gifted ball player whose dribbling skills and passing ability, when allied to a regular supply of goals, greatly enhanced Hibs' play in the time he was at the club. Russell's time at Rangers was not to be a success and although he extended his career, initially with Dundee United and then with Falkirk, there is no doubt that his best years in Scottish football were spent at Easter Road. It is just a shame that a popular player, who was both magical and magnificent, should leave Hibs under a cloud that was to a large extent of his own making.

Hibs run-up to the Scottish Cup Final, then, was not proceeding smoothly. Latapy was definitely out and there were doubts, too, over the club's other talisman, the great Franck Sauzée. For Franck to have missed the final would have been unthinkable and, thankfully, to the huge relief of the Hibs support, the medical bulletins coming out of Easter Road as the week progressed grew increasingly positive.

There was positivity among the Hibs fans, too, but it was mixed with a healthy dose of realism. How could it be anything else? Since last winning the cup, Hibs had contested and lost seven Scottish Cup Finals. It was not a record to engender complacency at the prospect of another tilt at the piece of silverware all Hibs supporters coveted most of all. Charlie Reid of the Proclaimers put things in context when he said, 'My dad used to tell me about Hibs winning the league three times after the war. I then asked him about the last time we had won the cup. He told me that that had been during the war. He didn't tell me, though, that he was talking about the Boer War!'

Other famous Hibees had something to say as well. Paul Kane remarked, 'There is a belief among the supporters that we are not just there to make up the numbers.' Jackie McNamara, whose son would play for Celtic at Hampden, had this message for the Hibs team: 'You will be legendary if you bring the cup back to Easter Road.' The great Joe Baker, who had played for Hibs in a Scottish Cup Final as a teenager, offered some sound advice to the players. 'Go out and enjoy it,' said Joe. 'These days don't come very often. You will remember it for ever.' Recently departed former captain John Hughes said wistfully, 'To be honest, I wish that I was part of it.' He then added, 'Hopefully they bring the cup home and that will do for me.'

As the big match approached, captain Franck Sauzée spoke. 'I have a good feeling about the cup this season. I am not blindly optimistic. I am a realist. I have a great respect for Celtic but I am not afraid,' was how Franck saw things. He went on to say, 'When we lost to Aberdeen in the semi-final last year, we were very disappointed but we learned a lot. When I speak to the players before the final, I will tell them it's a pleasure to be there.'

Franck then passed comments on the events surrounding Russell Latapy. He said, 'I am sad, of course, to see the wee man finish like that. We are men and sometimes we make mistakes. I think Russell realises that he has made mistakes. It's a shame but even if I love Russell, Alex McLeish has made the right decision at the right moment.'

Sauzée finished with, 'I am very proud to be club captain at a time when we have reached a national final. I don't think too many Frenchmen have had the honour of leading a team out in a Scottish Cup Final. It is a huge day for the club.'

It was indeed a massive day for Hibs but the club's supporters knew that they could not have a better man to skipper their side than Franck Sauzée. Franck's love for Hibernian seemed to grow with every day. He was a player of the highest class and had won the cup in France twice already in his career. He was also a highly inspirational individual.

The day of the Scottish Cup Final between Hibernian and Celtic, 26 May 2001, was a day of beautiful, warm, sunny weather. As the Hibernian support walked from their cars, buses and trains up to the national stadium, they had songs on their lips but tension in their stomachs.

'Could this really be the day?' they asked themselves, trying hard not to get too carried away with visions of the great Sauzée lifting gleaming silverware in front of them in a couple of hours' time. They also wondered whether this cup final day, like so many before it, would end in sadness and disappointment.

The first surprise was in Hibs' team selection. Stuart Lovell, who had played quietly but effectively all season, was replaced by young Ian Murray. McLeish had told Murray of his decision to play him on the Wednesday before the game. 'The boss had chosen me in a number of positions and when he called me to one side during the week, I honestly thought that he was going to tell me that I was on the bench,' recalls Murray now. 'When he said, "I'm going to muck you about again," I thought that that was definitely the case. However, he told me that I would be playing right wing back and I was delighted.' In the event, Alex McLeish's selection was vindicated as Murray had a good game. Lovell, though, must have felt intense disappointment.

Even now, the versatile and talented Lovell feels sadness at missing out on the final. 'Alex McLeish had told me to get a minor clean-up operation done on my knee before the semi-final against Livingston to make sure that I was ready for the final if we got there, so I couldn't believe it when he told me in the week leading up to the final that I wouldn't be playing. I asked him why I was being left out and he said that he thought Celtic might play Bobby Petta on the left wing and that he would cause me problems. I wonder now if it was because of the 5–2 league game leading up to the final. Lubo Moravcik weaved some of his magic on my side of the field that day and that may have been in the manager's mind.

'I argued my case with him and made the point that if he wanted me to constantly supplement the attack, there would be times when moves would break down and I would have to race back from a forward position. He couldn't have it both ways. I also said that I thought our best chance of beating Celtic was to go at them. However, Alex's mind was made up and he wasn't going to change it.

'I had to phone friends and family down South who were planning on coming up for the final and tell them that they might want to change their plans as I wasn't playing. It was my lowest time in football. My chin was really on the floor. In the event, Celtic didn't play Petta. He wasn't even on the bench, in fact. I don't hold Alex McLeish's selection against him, though. He did what he thought was right for the team and it was nothing personal. I may not agree with his decision but I accept it.'

When the match got under way, Hibs initially held their own. They looked to attack Celtic whenever possible and were creative without being greatly threatening. Reassuringly, there weren't too many alarms at the back. Then, as half time approached, the match took a decisive turn in Celtic's favour. A momentary lapse of concentration in the Hibs defence allowed Jackie McNamara in to open the scoring. One can only hazard a guess at what must have been going through McNamara's father's mind as he sat in the stand wearing a Hibs scarf. Ironically, McNamara had come on as a substitute to replace the gifted Lubo Moravcik. Most Hibs fans were glad to see the back of Moravcik but McNamara's entrance was to be crucial.

The confidence Hibs had displayed to that point must have been fragile because McNamara's goal seemed to take away their belief. Without ever being outclassed, Hibs were second best for the rest of the game. Two further goals from Henrik Larsson, the second of which was a debatable penalty awarded by referee Kenny Clark, finished the match as a contest.

John O'Neil, for one, feels that Hibs competed well in the match. He says, 'We were well in the game until Celtic scored. The final was evenly poised until then. Their second goal early in the second half made it hard for us but we didn't play badly. It still rankles with me that we didn't take our chance to win the Scottish Cup for Hibs. I don't lie awake at night thinking about it but I have to admit that it does come into my head from time to time that we all could have been Hibernian immortals. We definitely gave it our best shot, though.'

The huge Hibs support took their latest disappointment with dignity and returned to Edinburgh in crestfallen silence. As they did so, they reflected on their captain's performance. Franck Sauzée had clearly not been fully fit. There just hadn't been time for the injury he had bravely sustained against Rangers less than a week earlier to heal properly. This had prevented him from imposing his usual significant influence on the game. Speaking recently, Alex McLeish was honest enough to concede that his skipper had still been feeling the effects of his injury on cup final day. 'How could I leave him out, though?' asked McLeish. 'If Franck hadn't played, the rest of the team would have been completely deflated.' Hibs' former manager was absolutely right. Sauzée had to play. It was just Alex McLeish's and Hibs' misfortune that the great man had been injured in the last match before the cup final.

Nick Colgan, too, remembers knowing that Franck Sauzée wasn't at full fitness on cup final day. 'I don't think Franck would have played if it had been any other game but he put his body on the line for the club and the fans. Franck was definitely not able to command the game as much as he usually did. I still think that if we had kept the scores level until half time, we might have won the game and become all-time Hibee heroes. It wasn't to be, though, and another group of players will have to step up in future and attain immortality.'

Alex McLeish is now of the opinion that if he was playing that match against Celtic again, he would approach it differently. Instead of playing an open game and trying to match Celtic in style of play, Alex would now adopt tactics not dissimilar to those that he used so successfully when he steered Birmingham City to their historic Carling Cup triumph over Arsenal at Wembley. 'I would play more tightly this time,' says McLeish, 'and look to hit Celtic on the counter attack. I think that would be more effective.'

He is almost certainly correct again. Sadly, there are no second chances with cup finals. In truth, it probably wouldn't have mattered what Hibs had done on the day. They were unlucky enough to come up against a talented, resurgent Celtic team at the top of its game. The loss of Latapy and the injury to Sauzée had also severely dented Hibs' hopes. The fact is that, once more, the fates had conspired against Hibernian as they strove to attain their Holy Grail of the Scottish Cup.

The author and all of his close family attended the final with grandiose pre-match plans for lavish after-game celebrations. They all, of course, had to be forgotten about. Having been through this experience before in 1958, 1972 and 1979 didn't make it any easier to take. A suggestion was made that it would be a good idea to go down to Easter Road on returning to Edinburgh to welcome back the Hibs team. They had given their all and deserved to have that recognised. It would also give the evening a sense of purpose because, frankly, everyone was depressed and at a complete loss as to what to do next.

After arriving at Easter Road, there was not long to wait before the Hibs coach pulled up at the stadium. The team captain was first off the bus. The intention was to console him and thank him for his efforts but he spoke first. He said that he and the players were sorry that they had not won the cup and that they all really appreciated the support the Hibs fans had given them. He finished by saying, 'Maybe we will win the cup next year.'

These warm, comforting words, delivered in Franck's magnificent French accent made everyone feel much better. It is a pity that many other suffering Hibees were not there to hear them, too, and feel better as a result.

The players went into the ground to have a low-key celebration of a very successful season. They may not have won the cup but they had much to be proud of at the end of a highly successful season. Ian Murray had mixed feelings. 'I was broken hearted that we hadn't brought the cup home but I was happy with how I had played and with the fact that my family had been able to sit in the stand at Hampden and watch me play in a Scottish Cup Final for Hibs. We had such a good team then that I honestly thought that it was only a matter of time before we came back to Hampden and won the cup.'

When supporters of Hibernian FC woke the next morning, the scale of their disappointment probably matched the magnitude of their hangovers. As they went through the day, though, rational thought would have returned as dismay began to recede. They would have reflected that there was still much to be optimistic about. Another season was just around the corner and their team, once again led by Franck Sauzée, would be playing in Europe. There was very definitely light at the end of the tunnel. Not one of them could possibly have anticipated just what a cataclysmic campaign lay in wait for them.

11

FINAL FLING IN EUROPE

THE SUMMER of 2001, as all close seasons seem to do, passed very quickly. Alex McLeish was once again active in the transfer market and, as had been the case twelve months earlier, some familiar faces were leaving Hibs.

Russell Latapy was now a Rangers player. His presence and influence at Easter Road would be sorely missed. Stuart Lovell had also been allowed to move on. This was perhaps a little surprising as, after making a slow start in Scotland at the beginning of Hibs' promotion season, Lovell had won the fans over and, with his non-stop running and eye for goal, had become an important member of the first team squad.

Lovell had signed for newly promoted and highly ambitious Livingston. He would have preferred to stay with Hibs but the offer he was looking for hadn't been forthcoming. 'I wanted a three year deal but I was only offered a two year contract. I got the feeling that Alex McLeish had me in mind as a squad player for the next couple of seasons. I didn't want that. I was only twenty-nine and I wanted to be playing every week.

'Livingston offered me a three year deal and more money and Davie Hay, their manager, promised to play me in central midfield, so I accepted the terms which they had put on the table. When I told my dad that I was leaving Hibs, he was really disappointed. He said, "But you'll be playing in Europe." I pointed out to him that the team would be playing in Europe but that, if I stayed, I would probably be sitting on the bench watching them. In the event, I had three good years at Livingston at a time when they were successful. I even played in their team which beat Hibs in the 2004 League Cup Final. That was a funny feeling I can tell you. It was great to win a cup but I didn't want it to be against Hibs. Hibs had a huge support that day and the Livingston players were worried about it before the game. I reminded them that they were playing the opposing team not the crowd.

'I left Hibs with great memories and was really sad to do so. Funnily enough, I came up against Alex McLeish as manager four times that season and Livingston won every time. I have to say that Alex was a great manager to play for and there was a really nice message from him waiting for me when I arrived at Livingston.'

Dirk Lehmann was another who had headed for pastures new. He had returned to the South of England and joined up with Brighton. There was much sadness at the departure of Mixu Paatelainen. The big man had moved to France to play with Strasbourg, a former club of both Franck Sauzée and David Zitelli. Given that he had notched a double-figure tally of goals in the previous season, Paatelainen might have expected to be offered another contract. Alex McLeish obviously considered that he needed to freshen up his striking department. Mixu left with the best wishes of everyone at Easter Road. Ironically, he would join up with Hibs again just one season later.

Another forward who had gone through the exit door was Marc Libbra. Hibs would have loved to keep him. Celtic were also keen to sign Libbra but he chose to move to Norwich, where he got off to a flying start with a hat trick on his debut in a pre-season friendly match.

There were arrivals to balance the departures. A new goalkeeper arrived in the shape of Tony Caig who had been released by Charlton. The versatile 6 feet 5 inches tall Derek Townsley came from Motherwell. Townsley had played both sweeper and outside left against Hibs in the previous season, so he was clearly comfortable in a number of positions. Two strikers had come in, too. Craig Brewster returned from a sojourn with Ionikos in Greece. He had done well in Athens and had stayed there long enough to become his club's all-time top goal scorer. The other centre forward was the Spaniard, Francisco Javier Aguilera Blanco Luna. Scottish football commentators would be relieved to learn that he preferred to be known simply as 'Paco'.

Hibs had also signed two right backs, which probably confirms Stuart Lovell's suspicion that his days as a first team regular were numbered. Bosnian Alen Orman could also play in midfield and it looked like he would have to, as the other full back coming in was Hibs record signing, Ulises De la Cruz. De la Cruz had forty-two caps for Ecuador and had cost Hibs close to three-quarters of a million pounds if the newspaper estimates of his transfer fee were accurate. This was an enormous sum of money for a club like Hibs but a clear indication that, at that time, the board was prepared to speculate to accumulate. It is fair to say that the support of Sir Tom Farmer played a significant part in making this deal possible.

Alex McLeish had watched De la Cruz play and score against Brazil and had clearly been impressed by him. Then Hibs chairman Malcolm McPherson tells an amusing story about De la Cruz's signing. The club took the player, his advisers and an interpreter to a city centre hotel for a meal. It was mid-June and warm but De la Cruz was wearing a leather flying jacket with a fur collar.

Conversation was proving a little difficult until the full back whispered something in the interpreter's ear. She then turned to Mr McPherson and said, 'Ulises wants to know if it is always this cold in Scotland in the winter!'

Some people were also wondering whether Franck Sauzée was starting to turn his thoughts to a career in coaching or management. Stuart Lovell had this to say: 'Franck has a great knowledge of the game and he is a fantastic role model for young players. I don't think it would be a bad move to groom him for the manager's job.' Given what was to follow, Lovell's views were to prove remarkably prescient.

At that time, though, Sauzée's thoughts were solely on playing. He had returned to the South of France during the summer to have blood tests conducted by his doctor. Franck apparently underwent this analysis at the start of every season to ensure that the levels of iron, magnesium and other substances in his body were exactly as they should be. Duly tested, he professed himself in excellent shape and fully ready for the fray.

Hibs' pre-season preparations took them to France and it was a sentimental journey for Sauzée, as the first game on their trip was against Marseille, the club where he had enjoyed so much success earlier in his career. The match was played in Arzon, a small coastal town in Brittany, as part of the Bastille Day celebrations. Hibs outplayed Marseille and beat them 2–1 with goals from the newly recruited Orman and young Garry O'Connor. The French side certainly took the game seriously and adopted a physical approach that wasn't to Alex McLeish's liking.

At full time, the crowd invaded the pitch. They ran straight past their own players, including their latest big money signings, and made straight for Franck Sauzée. It took Franck some time to extricate himself from the adoring throng – he had clearly lost none of his popularity in his homeland.

Four hundred Hibs fans had travelled across for the game and in the course of the day of the match, the hostelries in Arzon had sold as much beer as they would normally do in a complete season. It wasn't just Marseille supporters who wanted to get close to Franck Sauzée after the match either. One Hibee was proudly carrying a French national flag, which he asked Sauzée to sign. Franck, naturally, obliged. It was just as well that he didn't ask where the flag had come from. The Hibs fan in question had climbed up the flagpole on the ferry during his cross-Channel journey and claimed his prize without regard to either his own safety or any niceties relating to legal ownership.

On their return home, Hibs would have continued their French theme by experiencing a sensation of déjà vu in advance of their opening league fixture. The computer had paired them with

Kilmarnock at Easter Road. As the two sides had met six times in the previous season, there would be no lack of familiarity between them.

When captain Sauzée led Hibs out, he was welcomed by an enthusiastic crowd of just under 13,000, many of whom were seated in the newly completed and highly impressive West Stand. It was a marvellous game. An uncharacteristic Sauzée slip allowed Michel Ngonge to give Kilmarnock the lead. Franck soon righted that wrong with a thunderous penalty kick into the roof of the Killie net.

The Ayrshire men went ahead again but sustained Hibs pressure was deservedly rewarded when Ulrik Laursen defied his prediction of the previous season about his goal-scoring capabilities by heading a late equaliser.

The match provided some clues to Alex McLeish's thinking as he sought to move his team forward. Gary Smith was left out and Ulrik Laursen was in central defence with Sauzée and Fenwick. With De la Cruz at right back as expected, Orman did indeed play in midfield. Brewster and Luna were up front with Zitelli moving into midfield. This new line-up looked good in attack with the speedy, skilful De la Cruz particularly catching the eye. Hibs were much less convincing defensively, though. Nonetheless, the *Daily Record* reporter at the game was moved to write, 'It may have been the opening day of the league programme but we will be hard pressed to find a more entertaining match all season.'

Hibs suffered a setback when they lost 2–1 to Dundee at Dens Park in their next game, but came back strongly to beat Aberdeen 2–0 and draw 2–2 with Rangers in the matches that followed. Sauzée was again on target from the penalty spot against the Dons and Hibs' other goal was supplied by the pacey Tom McManus. McManus then put Hibs ahead at Ibrox but it took a truly special second goal from Alen Orman to secure a point. Orman worked his way across the edge of the Rangers penalty area before wheeling and releasing a howitzer of a shot that ripped into the roof of the net. At this stage, Orman looked a tremendous signing. Unfortunately, he did not manage to fulfil his early promise.

There was another reverse when Celtic came to town. In a game that was uncannily similar to Celtic's 5–2 win at Easter Road prior to the previous season's Scottish Cup Final, Hibs proceeded to play attractive football but miss chances. Celtic, on the other hand, were once again clinical in their finishing and went in at half time 4–0 up. A late Paul Fenwick header restored some respectability for Hibs but was, in truth, scant consolation to the disappointed home support. They agreed with their captain when he said after the game, 'We have things to work on.'

The draw for the opening round of the UEFA Cup had been made and Hibs were playing a strong and accomplished European team in AEK Athens. The first leg of the tie, which would be held in Greece, was not far away and Alex McLeish was looking for his team to find some form before the game took place. They did exactly that winning successive matches against Motherwell and Dunfermline, 3–1 and 5–1 respectively.

In the game at Fir Park, McLeish restored the central defensive partnership of Smith, Fenwick and Sauzée. Hibs looked much the better for this move and played well. Their inspirational skipper scored two goals. He converted a first half penalty with typical aplomb but when referee Stuart Dougal awarded Hibs a second spot kick, he uncharacteristically failed to score.

Current Hibs stalwart, Ian Murray, remembers the Motherwell game well. 'When we came in at half time, Franck was furious with himself for missing the second penalty. He looked us all in the eye and said, "I should not miss a penalty kick. If we get a free kick on the edge of the box after half time, I am taking it and it is going straight into the top left-hand corner of the net." He clearly meant every word that he said and none of us doubted for a minute that he would keep his promise.

'Sure enough, we got a free kick on the edge of the Motherwell penalty area in the second half. Franck stepped up and we all knew exactly what was going to happen. He was as good as his word and curled the ball beautifully into the top corner. It was a great goal by a great player and showed not just his ability as a footballer but his mental strength as well.'

If Sauzée had scored with both penalty kicks, he would have notched his one and only Hibs hat trick. Sadly, it wasn't to be. However, with four goals from six starts, he was doing not at all badly for a central defender.

Dunfermline were also comfortably disposed of, with Brewster and Luna both scoring twice and McManus adding the other. Alex McLeish was full of praise for Hibs after this game and now felt more optimistic about the imminent trip to Athens. *The Scotsman* agreed. Its correspondent wrote, 'As preparations for Europe go, this was just about perfect for Hibs.'

Franck Sauzée recalled travelling to Greece to play AEK with Marseille. He explained how the French team's bus had been hit with stones and bricks and described the experience as the 'worst welcome' of his football career. Franck's fitness for the upcoming match was in doubt, as Dunfermline's Dutch striker, Jack de Gier, had injured Franck's Achilles tendon with a mistimed challenge.

Hibs' game in the Greek capital had been delayed due to the terrorist attacks on New York, which had taken place on Tuesday, 11 September 2001. The game had originally been scheduled for Thursday, 13 September. The Hibs team's plane had been stopped on the airport runway just before take-off as news of the terrible events in the USA had begun to filter through.

Significant numbers of Hibs supporters had already left for Athens. They had no match to watch but enjoyed themselves anyway. Many of them returned a week later when the game eventually took place.

There was a major blow for Hibs when their captain was unable to take his normal place in defence due to his Achilles injury. The temperature was well above eighty degrees Fahrenheit and the accompanying high humidity didn't make things any easier for the Easter Road men. In the event, despite the hostile atmosphere generated by a noisy and volatile crowd, they acquitted themselves creditably and were unfortunate to return with a 2–0 defeat. A harshly awarded penalty had not helped their cause either. The players all felt that they could still win the tie overall at Easter Road. Ian Murray was impressed by a stirring post-match talk that Alex McLeish gave to his players. 'When we got back into the dressing room in Athens, the boss sat us down and told us that he was sure we would do enough at home to go through to the next round. He spoke to us for half an hour and he was inspirational. By the time he was finished, we couldn't wait for the second leg.'

Hibs travelled home in the early hours of Friday morning and were back in league action against St Johnstone on the Sunday afternoon. In the light of their exertions, a 4–0 home win was highly commendable. Sauzée was still absent but goals from Fenwick (his third in four games), Luna, Allan Smart (a new loan signing from Watford) and a rejuvenated Grant Brebner, gave Hibs a rare convincing victory over the Perth side, which then, as now, usually made life difficult for Hibs. The stage was now set for the return visit of AEK Athens, with Hibs supporters of a mature vintage hoping for a repeat of some of the great European nights that they had experienced in their youth.

Alex McLeish had constantly praised the Hibs support during his time as club manager. There was no doubt that they had bought into what the manager was trying to achieve and felt that their team, after some years in the doldrums, was on the verge of something special. McLeish asked the fans for an extra effort in the game against AEK Athens. He said, 'We have never needed your backing more than we do tonight.' He displayed powers of clairvoyance when he added, 'A momentous night might be on the cards.'

When AEK Athens met Hibernian from the Athens of the North, an unforgettable evening ensued. The atmosphere was incredible and the noise was stupendous. The singing of 'Sunshine on Leith' at half time raised the hairs on the back of every Hibee's neck.

The game was exciting, with Hibs' performance more than doing the occasion justice. Franck Sauzée was back and he produced an immense display. His colleagues weren't far behind him, not least De la Cruz, whose right wing runs ripped through the Greek defence time and again.

Paco Luna scored twice and, with a minute of the match remaining, he had the opportunity to write himself into Hibs history forever. Presented with a free header at the far post, Luna saw his effort slide agonisingly past. This didn't dilute Hibs' optimism as they entered extra time. However, two strikes by AEK did.

The first was a long shot, which Nick Colgan got a hand to but couldn't keep out. The second Greek goal entered Hibs' net from a corner after taking an unfortunate flick off Paul Fenwick's head. A Zitelli special flew past the AEK goalkeeper to give Hibs victory on the night but sadly, and undeservedly, they were out on aggregate.

A turning point may have been Franck Sauzée's departure from the field with a head injury in the second half. The depth of Franck's disappointment at having to leave the pitch could be measured by the furious kick that the normally urbane Frenchman gave the Hibs dugout as he took his dejected seat on the bench. The noise reverberated all the way round Easter Road.

After the game, Alex McLeish was strongly of the opinion that Hibs should have been in the draw for the next round. He said, 'We combined great passion with excellent technical play. We won the battle but not the war.'

Young Ian Murray, who had played a full part in the inspired display against AEK, said, 'It was the biggest noise I have ever heard at Easter Road. It was sensational to play on such a night. I was devastated that we had lost when we deserved to win but I was proud of how we had played. We were nothing short of brilliant and if Paco's header had gone in, we would have recorded a great victory. Although we didn't know it at the time, that game almost signalled the end of an era, as Franck stopped playing not long afterwards and things were never the same again.'

Nick Colgan shared his team mate's feelings. 'What a night that was. The singing of "Sunshine on Leith" as we came out after half time was incredible. I will take that experience to the grave with me. The Greeks told us after the game that they couldn't believe the pace we played at and the fact that we sustained that level of commitment for ninety minutes. Paco's header was the turning point. If he had scored, the game was ours. Sadly, he put it just past the post.'

Hibs suffered a reaction to their unlucky exit from the UEFA Cup by losing successive away matches in the league at Livingston, who were fourth in the league and doing extremely well, and Dundee United. Sauzée was unfit for the first match and, as always, the absence of the captain and fulcrum of the team was keenly felt.

There was a comfortable 2–0 win against Raith Rovers at Stark's Park in the League Cup to cheer up Hibs fans. Craig Brewster scored two fine goals and Hibs hit the frame of the goal no less than five times.

Next came the first Edinburgh derby of the season. This was Ulises De la Cruz's day. The Ecuadorian enigma was still looking suspect in defence and nobody could say that his work rate was phenomenal, but he was magnificent going forward. He had pace and skill and usually delivered a dangerous cross. Against Hearts, he decided to show his shooting prowess. With barely a minute on the clock, he cut inside and unleashed a long distance shot that buried itself in the Hearts net. De la Cruz added a second from much closer range – around two feet perhaps – later in the half to put Hibs in command.

Craig Brewster was really fired up for his first derby and, having already been booked, was removed by his manager before half time just in case he got himself sent off. Brewster wasn't best pleased at the time but admitted after the game that his manager had got it right.

Grant Brebner, who was having a fine season, had an outstanding game and the positive influence of fit-again Franck Sauzée was there for all to see. One report even described his performance as 'world class'. Hibs conceded a second half goal and allowed Hearts back into the game but there was never really any prospect of the visitors saving the match.

At full time, Hibs fans leaving the stadium in torrential rain could reflect that it was exactly 364 days since the historic 6–2 victory over the same opponents the previous autumn. They would also be happy with the form of two of their younger players. In a Scottish Youth Cup tie against Annan Athletic, Hibs had won 10–0 with Derek Riordan scoring five goals and Garry O'Connor contributing four.

The match that followed against Dundee at home was a frustrating exercise for Hibs. They dominated the game but missed chance after chance. With the game locked at 1–1, Franck Sauzée, striving to win the game for his team, surged forward at every opportunity. As chances were created and missed, Alex McLeish, on the touchline, fell to his knees in exasperation. The inevitable happened when Steven Milne scored the winning goal in the last minute with what was only Dundee's second shot at goal in the match.

Franck Sauzée suffered a recurrence of his Achilles tendon injury in this game and was once again out of action. Although no one knew it at the time, the Gallic God had, in fact, played his last match for Hibs.

Hibs once more struggled without their inspirational captain and lost to Aberdeen after drawing, yet again, with Kilmarnock. Hibs fans were becoming concerned about the severity of their skipper's injury but Franck, now turned thirty-six years old, had reassuring words for them. He said, 'I have had no thoughts of stopping playing. I remain a footballer and I am 100% focused on playing. Hibernian supporters can rest assured that all my energies are devoted to playing. I know the fans are desperate to see me back but I must not rush things. Things are a little difficult just now and the temptation is to return quickly but I know that I am no use to the team unless I am fully fit.'

In an attempt to improve his team's fortunes, Alex McLeish sold defender Martin McIntosh to Rotherham and brought in centre forward Eduardo Hurtado from Ulises De la Cruz's homeland of Ecuador. Hurtado had good credentials, having scored forty-three

121

goals in seventy-one matches for his country. At well over six feet tall and weighing in at fourteen stones, he was nicknamed 'The Tank'. It has to be said that there was nothing remotely warlike about his performances in the weeks to follow.

Hibs' league form didn't get better. The replacement of Nick Colgan with Tony Caig didn't help matters either. Caig was less than impressive in a 3–0 home defeat to high-flying Livingston. A ray of light was a 2–0 League Cup quarter final win over Dundee United, with McManus and Luna on target. In what proved to be his last set of programme notes, Alex McLeish spoke of 'a semi-final tie to look forward to'. Hibs had, in fact, been paired with First Division Ayr United but by the time that game came round in February of the following year, the manager would have been gone from Hibs for quite some time.

Another league reverse to Celtic at Parkhead meant that Hibs had only taken four points from seven matches. One newspaper described the club's problem as 'Third Force Syndrome' and made the point that they were suffering a reaction to the previous season's exertions and success. A simpler theory was that, without Latapy and Sauzée, they were a mere shadow of the team that these two outstanding players had graced. Franck, in fact, was still Hibs' top league scorer with four goals when eighteen games had been played. Due to injury, he had only managed to play in ten of these games and hadn't been able to complete all of them. Hibs sat in eighth place in the league table.

Hurtado made his debut in an unimpressive 1–1 draw at home to Motherwell, a game in which Hibs conceded another late goal. That disappointment was nothing compared to the emotions felt by everyone connected with Hibs when it emerged after the game that Rangers had approached Alex McLeish to replace Dick Advocaat as their manager.

McLeish wanted to accept the challenge of taking over at Ibrox and Hibs didn't stand in his way. It would be fair to say that there were some very bruised feelings at Easter Road. Malcolm McPherson, who was Hibs chairman at that time, remembers,

'I felt very hurt and let down at Alex leaving us the way he did. We had shown loyalty to him and expected the same in return.' McPherson admits that he 'fell out' with McLeish over his sudden departure. He says now, 'Alex did a fine job as manager of Hibs and he restored pride to the club. I was disappointed at the way he left. However, he is a big man in more ways than one. Some time after his departure, we were both at the same football dinner. Alex walked across the room to my table and hugged me. That was an action typical of the man. Happily, our friendship has been restored.'

Alex McLeish himself said recently, 'I was very happy at Hibs and retain an affection for the club. I think I did a good job during my time at Easter Road. I understood Hibs supporters being angry with me at the time. That's the way human nature works. I would hope, though, that if I went back to a Hibs game now, people would make me welcome and react positively towards me. Time is a great healer.'

The coolness that Alex McLeish's career move to Rangers created in the higher echelons of Easter Road was reflected in the match programme for the first home game after he had left. The fixture list, in the fatalistic way it often does, had thrown up a visit from McLeish's new employers. There was no warm message acknowledging McLeish's achievements with Hibs and wishing him well in his new post. The only reference to the change in Hibs' management structure was a terse sentence that read, 'In a whirlwind move, Alex McLeish and his assistant Andy Watson were one minute the management team at Easter Road, the next installed at Rangers.'

The sense of hurt and rejection that prevailed in the Hibernian community after Alex McLeish's dramatic change of allegiance was completely understandable. It was also, in truth, based on the realisation that Hibs had lost an excellent young manager who would be extremely difficult to replace.

12

MANAGER OF HIBS

THE DAY after Alex McLeish's departure from Hibs was officially confirmed, he sat in the stand at Ibrox to watch his old team take on his new charges. Dick Advocaat was in the Rangers dugout for the last time and Youth Coach Donald Park took temporary charge of Hibs. The Hibees made a point and gained a point in a creditable 1–1 draw but, unusually for a Hibs v Rangers game, the action on the field was overshadowed by events off it.

Speculation on who would succeed McLeish was rife. One newspaper poll showed very clearly how the Hibs supporters felt. Offered the opportunity to vote for candidates such as Tommy Burns, Murdo MacLeod, David Hay or Ian McCall, 80% of Hibs fans ignored them and nominated Franck Sauzée as the man they wanted in charge of their club.

Franck was in France recuperating from his Achilles tendon injury but returned to Edinburgh on hearing of Alex McLeish's resignation. Hibs were spoiled for choice when it came to replacing McLeish. Malcolm McPherson recently confirmed that they had received well over a hundred applications for the manager's post at Easter Road and many of those promoting their candidacy were of a very high calibre in terms of experience and expertise.

Hibs Chief Executive, Rod Petrie, met with Franck Sauzée. Their discussion went well. In the course of it, Franck looked Petrie in the eye and said, as only he could, 'I am ready.' When Petrie reported back to his board of directors, they didn't take long to make a decision. They decided that Sauzée was their man and that he should be offered the job of manager. It is clear that Franck was keen to accept their offer as his negotiations with Rod Petrie lasted for no more than five minutes.

Three short days after Alex McLeish had walked out of Easter Road, Franck Sauzée became the manager of Hibernian Football Club. His appointment met with almost universal approval. Franck had asked for Donald Park as his assistant and Rod Petrie, at the press conference to unveil them, introduced Sauzée and Park as a 'dream team'.

After Sauzée's appointment and prior to the press conference, there had been media speculation as to whether Franck would be a player-manager or simply concentrate on the management side of things. He made his intentions clear immediately when he said, 'You cannot do two jobs, so I have decided to end my playing career. Franck Sauzée as a player is now history.' Sauzée stressed that he was not stopping playing because of his injury, which was healing well. He simply did not want anything to get in the way of his career as manager.

Writing in the *Edinburgh Evening News*, David Hardie described Sauzée as 'the most celebrated player in the club's recent history' and wondered if his sudden retirement had taken the Hibs board by surprise. Malcolm McPherson said that this was not the case. He stated, 'We know that Franck was struggling with injury and we weren't too surprised when he announced that he was giving up playing.'

Sauzée was characteristically honest when he spoke to the press and media for the first time as manager of Hibs. 'I have a name as a player,' he said, 'but I may be the worst manager you have ever seen in Scotland.'

When asked if Sauzée had pushed the directors for funds for new players, Malcolm McPherson explained, 'All he said was that he wanted the job. He loves the club.' It seemed like a lot of people loved Franck Sauzée, too. The Hibs support was euphoric at his appointment. Former player Stuart Lovell was full of praise when he declared, 'Franck has achieved so much in his career yet he is a humble, modest man who doesn't shout about it from the rooftops. He will have no problems dealing with the players.' Even Alex McLeish weighed in with, 'Franck was an inspirational player with great experience, which is obviously going to help. He is a good friend and I know well the quality of the man.'

It had turned out, then, that Franck Sauzée's last game as a Hibs player had been in the unlucky 2–1 defeat to Dundee a few weeks earlier. This could only be regarded as an anti-climactic swansong. As the great man himself put it, 'I did not realise then that my career had stopped.'

No one was dwelling on the past, though. There was an exciting new future in prospect. Sauzée ended his inaugural press conference by stating, 'The past three years have been fantastic. As a player with Hibs, I have probably had the best period of my career.' Given the huge success Franck had enjoyed prior to coming to Easter Road, this was a truly significant statement.

He went on to say, 'I want my players to be happy. If I did not love them, I would not have taken the job. I spoke to the players before my appointment was announced and told them that it was important that they forgot about me as a player and did it themselves.' This statement was romantic and idealistic – not many football managers talk about loving their players after all – but all the better for being just that. Here was a man who was going to eschew the hard-bitten, pragmatic approach adopted by most team managers and do it his way. The big question was: would that way be successful?

There is no doubt that Sauzée's appointment was popular with the players who had been his team mates until his change of status. Ian Murray recalls, 'All the players wanted Franck to get the job and we were delighted when he did. He sat us down in the dressing room half an hour before he went out to meet the media and told us that he was the new manager. We couldn't have been happier.

We all had huge respect for Franck and wanted him to succeed. The last thing we wanted to do was to let him down.'

The first stage of Franck Sauzée's managerial journey took him across the Forth Road Bridge to Dunfermline the day after his appointment had been made public. He was joined by thousands of Hibs supporters who, like their new boss, travelled with hope in their hearts. He gave his first team talk to his players in a Fife hotel after they had finished their pre-match meal. Ian Murray remembers it well. 'It was an excellent talk. He made us all feel great. It was clear that Franck's attitude as a manager was that it was all about the players rather than himself.'

At two minutes to three on Saturday, 15 December 2001, Franck Sauzée emerged from the tunnel at East End Park and walked down the track towards the technical area. He was dressed in a beautifully tailored black overcoat and exuded an aura of class. The Hibs support, at the far end of the ground, rose to him and applauded his every step to the dugout. Some of the fans may even have had tears in their eyes. The author of this book most certainly did.

Sadly, Sauzée's managerial debut was not successful. Dougie McDonald, the referee, sent off Paco Luna in twenty-seven minutes and Hibs' ten men, try as they might, could not prevent Dunfermline from securing a slightly fortuitous 1–0 win. Franck gained his first point the following Saturday from a hard fought 0–0 draw with St Johnstone at McDiarmid Park. Hibs' next game was on Boxing Day. Rangers would be the visitors to Easter Road and Sauzée would get an early opportunity to pit his wits against the man who had brought him to Hibs – Alex McLeish.

This was, of course, Franck Sauzée's first home game as Hibs manager and, it is fair to say, that the welcomes he and his opposing manager received were of a contrasting nature.

Franck had this to say in his first set of managerial notes in the match programme: 'I genuinely love this club. I feel a deep sense of attachment to the players and fans here at Easter Road. I consider it an honour to manage such a wonderful club. I want my players to show the same love and desire for Hibernian that the fans show.'

This was marvellous stuff. Sauzée's favourite four-letter word had been employed again and the sincerity of his feelings for Hibs was unmistakeable. No Hibs player or manager could ever have felt closer to the club's supporters nor had their feelings so warmly reciprocated.

Still, Sauzée's elusive first victory would not come. Rangers ran out winners by the flattering score of 3–0. Their margin of victory was boosted by two late goals and the game was engulfed by what *The Scotsman* described as 'the flames of controversy'. The man in the middle of the contentious goings-on was referee Mike McCurry. When Ulrik Laursen blocked a shot on the line, McCurry decided that the ball had struck his hand and awarded a penalty. He then ordered off Laursen for denying Rangers a goal-scoring opportunity. Most people thought that the referee's decision was harsh. Tom McManus certainly did and disputed the spot kick award. McCurry responded by sending him off, too.

All of this not only helped Rangers to achieve an ultimately comfortable victory, it also created serious problems for Franck Sauzée as he prepared to take his team to Tynecastle for the festive derby three days later. Hibs already had a lengthy injury list to contend with and now two players were also suspended.

Those Hibs fans who feared the worst should have known better. Franck Sauzée had never lost a derby match to Hearts and he didn't intend to start now. Franck had appointed John O'Neil to replace himself as captain. He had also awarded long-term contracts to the two eighteen-year-old strikers Garry O'Connor and Derek Riordan. This was to prove a commendable piece of management. Both players became fans' favourites and, in due course, were sufficiently successful to earn big money moves. Happily, both saw the light and returned to Easter Road at a later date.

All three of these players were to make their mark at Tynecastle. O'Connor started the match and caused the Hearts defence plenty of problems with his direct style. Riordan came on as a substitute and made a very favourable impression, and skipper O'Neil gained Hibs a fighting 1–1 draw with a sweetly struck shot in the ninetieth minute of the match. Franck Sauzée had now taken on Hearts nine times as a Hibernian player and manager and was yet to lose a game.

The Hibs match programme for the next home match against Dundee United commented on Riordan's new five-year deal by saying, 'We will be hearing and reading a lot more about young Derek in future.' They weren't wrong. In truth, he and O'Connor had already got the fans talking.

In the Scottish Youth Cup, they and their under-18 colleagues had followed up the ten-goal rout of Annan with an exciting victory over Livingston. Losing 4–2 in extra time, Hibs had come back to win 5–4. O'Connor had contributed a hat trick and Riordan had also been on the score sheet. Kevin Thomson had scored Hibs' other goal and Steven Whittaker had played well in defence. There was clearly no shortage of youthful talent at Easter Road.

Franck Sauzée would have been hoping to build on the derby draw when Dundee United first-footed Hibs on 2 January 2002. Sauzée's team played well but failed to take their chances. United made them pay for this with a last-minute goal that was very much against the run of play.

Hibs had no time to feel sorry for themselves as the games came thick and fast. Next up was a trip to Stair Park for a Scottish Cup match with Stranraer. The good form shown against Dundee United wasn't replicated and Hibs could only manage an extremely disappointing 0–0 draw. There was another defeat in the league at Dens Park, where Freddy Arpinon didn't help his team by getting himself sent off.

Things were not going well. To be fair to Franck Sauzée, they hadn't been going that well before he had taken control of the team. Since the 2–1 derby victory over Hearts on 21 October, Hibs had played thirteen matches. They had lost eight of them and drawn the other five.

The manager was philosophical in his programme notes before the replay with Stranraer. He said, 'Against Dundee United, we saw the story of the whole season played out in one single match. We played very well but couldn't score and a late goal sunk us.' He then praised the Hibs support, which was still 100% behind the new manager, saying, 'I am very proud and humbled by the backing we have received from our fans during this difficult time. You have remained behind us while results have gone against us.'

The players were behind their manager, too. Ian Murray says, 'We were really enjoying working with Franck. In many ways, he was ahead of his time as a manager. When he took over, he said, "If you are over twenty-one, call me Franck. Otherwise, call me boss." He was very detailed tactically and training was very passing orientated. He was trying to get us to play in the French way. We had some good players and we put in some decent performances, but the results just wouldn't come.'

Despite the team's poor form, almost 9,000 Hibs supporters braved the elements on a midweek night for the second Stranraer game. They got their reward when Manager Sauzée recorded his first victory in his eighth game in charge. It was a convincing one, too. Eduardo Hurtado and Gary Smith got their first goals for Hibs, while Paco Luna and David Zitelli also scored. *The Scotsman* summed up how most Hibs fans felt when it reported next day: 'Franck Sauzée has known many great victories in his career but few will have delivered as much relief and satisfaction as this one.'

Franck would have hoped to build on this cup success with his first league win and he should have got it in the next match. Hibs led Kilmarnock 2–0 well into the second half with Hurtado again on target.

Even when Kilmarnock pulled a goal back, Hibs, with Riordan and O'Connor on as substitutes and both playing extremely well, should have added to their lead. They failed to do so, though, and the inevitable happened when Kilmarnock snatched an unwarranted last-minute equaliser.

If the result hadn't been what manager Sauzée was looking for, then the performance had been. He said, 'I was happy with the attitude of my players and their performance. The signs are clear that we are improving.' No one who had watched the Kilmarnock game could have argued with that assessment and when Aberdeen came to Easter Road the following midweek, there was no lack of optimism.

Once again, though, the fates conspired against Hibs and Franck Sauzée. With Ulises De la Cruz in outstanding form on the right flank, Hibs played superbly in attack and created a host of chances. They even managed to convert three of them. Unfortunately, they defended in lamentable fashion and conceded three goals as well. As the match entered its final minute, most Hibs supporters were bemoaning the fact that it looked like they would have to accept yet another draw from a game that should have been won. At that point, referee Hugh Dallas stepped in and awarded the softest of penalties against Ian Murray. Even then, Nick Colgan saved Darren Young's spot kick but Darren Mackie, so often a scorer against Hibs over the years, followed up to tuck away the rebound and consign Hibs to a very unlucky 4–3 defeat.

Hibs were now second bottom of the SPL with only St Johnstone below them. To this point, Franck Sauzée had remained positive and supportive of his players. After the Aberdeen game, he got angry for the first time.

He said, 'Offensively, we were excellent. Defensively, I was annoyed by the bad mistakes we made. I am very, very upset.' Sauzée then added, with a large measure of understatement, 'I think it is fair to say that we are suffering a bit of bad luck at the moment. Late goals are destroying us.' There was little argument with the manager's summary of events. Hibs had been hit by a series of injuries and suspensions. They had also been on the receiving end of refereeing decisions and had conceded damaging goals late in games.

There were scraps of encouragement for Sauzée, though. A young player called Scott Brown had just moved up from the under-16 team to the under-18s and was earning rave reviews. Here, then, was another player for Hibs' future. Franck would also be happy that he was no longer the club's top scorer in league games. With his two goals against Aberdeen, Paco Luna, on 23 January, had at last overtaken the manager who hadn't played since the previous October. Finally, Sauzée knew that he still had the backing of the Hibs support, as almost 11,000 had turned out for the Aberdeen game on a very wet Wednesday night.

There was no respite for Hibs' beleaguered boss as he had to take his team to Ibrox for a Scottish Cup tie against Rangers just three days after the reverse to the Dons. A first half Grant Brebner goal gave Hibs brief hope but, in the end, Rangers ran out comfortable 4–1 winners.

The realities of managerial life were now sinking in for Franck Sauzée. As a player, he had enjoyed going to art galleries with his artist wife Guylaine. Now he had no time for such pleasures. As one journalist put it, 'Sauzée's priority is now professionalism rather than expressionism.'

Franck was starting to feel the pressure. David Hardie of the *Edinburgh Evening News* recalls, 'I used to have a chat with Franck every day during his time as manager. At the start, he was happy and optimistic and spoke freely. As time wore on, though, he became more guarded and a little down. He started to look tired and strained as well.'

Franck admitted as much in an interview with one of the Sunday papers. He said, 'This is a different kind of stress. As a player, you just have to prepare your own game. As a manager, you have to think about all the players and worry about what happens if you lose. I'm tired after the games for mental reasons.'

Sauzée had approached his managerial career with cavalier thoughts in mind. Now he was more pragmatic as he stated, 'Playing for enjoyment is not enough. We are too soft. We were absolutely rubbish in parts of the Aberdeen game and I told the players so.'

Franck had played under such fine managers as Arsene Wenger, Gérard Houllier and Michel Platini. He now made it clear that he intended to contact his old bosses and pick their brains. More than anything, though, he needed to pick up points.

His next opportunity to do so came in a Saturday evening Sky Television match against Celtic. Sauzée had made a couple of signings. One of them, Finnish international midfielder Jarkko Wiss had played against Aberdeen without making a major impression.

Franck now brought in the young central defender Gary Caldwell from Newcastle United on loan. Caldwell would make his debut against the Parkhead men who were comfortable leaders of the SPL table. In the match programme, there was a feature on the pop music charts of previous years. Topping the list ten years earlier had been Kylie Minogue with 'Give Me Just a Little More Time'. Similar thoughts would almost certainly have been going through the mind of the Hibs manager.

His team did its best to help him. Hibs played outstandingly well and took the lead through young O'Connor. The big striker was in barnstorming form and was ably backed up by De la Cruz, whose speedy forays on the right flank caused Celtic no end of difficulties, and Caldwell, who gave a mature and impressive display at centre half. In the end, Hibs didn't manage to hold on to their lead as John Hartson scored a second half equaliser, but a 1–1 draw was a creditable result against a team that had come into the match with a thirteen-point lead over second-placed Rangers in the league table.

Franck Sauzée was pleased. He declared, 'This is the way we must play every week.' He was absolutely right. It had probably been Hibs' best performance under Sauzée's stewardship and Hibs fans would have been more than happy to see this standard of football and commitment maintained in every game. Even Celtic manager Martin O'Neill was moved to say, 'I am delighted for Franck Sauzée.'

He wasn't half as delighted as the Hibs supporters were though. They still backed their manager and were now looking forward with confidence to the League Cup semi-final match with Ayr United at Hampden, which was played four days later. The prospect of a cup final in the spring seemed very real and the Hibs fans who made up the vast majority of the crowd in the national stadium had travelled in the expectation of a repeat of the team's form from the Celtic match and a comfortable passage into the final. What they got was something completely different.

Hibs were dreadfully disappointing and never really took command of the game or threatened to score against an Ayr team that included players like John Hughes and Pat McGinlay, who had been deemed surplus to requirements at Easter Road.

The game went into extra time and, as the possibility of a penalty shoot-out started to ring alarm bells among the Hibs support, referee Mike McCurry took a hand. He awarded Ayr a penalty that could best be described as dubious and Eddie Annand dispatched the spot kick into the Hibs net.

Hibs never looked like mounting a comeback and, most worryingly of all, Franck Sauzée stood on the touchline looking like a man who wasn't sure what to do next. Franck wasn't really a man for bawling and shouting or gesturing and gesticulating but, on this occasion, his body language sent out a negative message to both his team and their supporters.

Sauzée was brutally honest after the match. 'There can be no excuses,' he said. 'The penalty award may have been harsh but ultimately the reason we lost the match was that we did not show enough fight or enough quality on the evening.' The manager finished by saying that he expected a massive reaction from his players when they visited Fir Park on league business at the weekend.

The players felt for Sauzée after the Ayr defeat. Ian Murray sums it up when he reflects, 'Our confidence was low at this time. Coming off the back of a really good display against Celtic, we should have beaten Ayr easily but we didn't. Don't ask me why. It could only have been a lack of self belief. That is what separated players like Franck and Russell from the rest of us. Apart from their talent, they were really strong mentally and could be at their best when it mattered most. We really felt for Franck after that Ayr game.'

Sadly, Hibs' manager did not get the response he was looking for when his team returned to league duty. Things got worse instead of better. Motherwell won by the embarrassing margin of 4–0 and Sauzée was again understandably downbeat in his post-match comments, describing the Hibs performance as 'a dreadful defeat and a humiliating reversal for the club.'

Sauzée was still looking for his first league win as manager when Dunfermline visited Easter Road seven days later. In his programme notes, he again paid tribute to the fans, saying, 'The last few weeks have been among the most depressing and frustrating we could imagine. Instead of looking forward to a cup final, we face the hard realities of a relegation battle. The supporters have been truly wonderful in a dreadful run of results. Now the players must show the same love, passion and desire for the club as these fans.'

This was vintage Franck Sauzée. He was, as always, speaking from the heart and effortlessly further strengthening the special bond that existed between him and the Hibernian support. Again he had spoken of the love for Hibs that he and the fans shared. The big question now was whether the players were equally committed to the club and ready to start to play to their potential.

The game against Dunfermline suggested otherwise. Hibs scrambled a less than impressive 1–1 draw with a late goal from Derek Townsley but the team's lack of confidence was there for all to see. There was no lack of effort, mind you. As *The Scotsman's* match report put it, 'Hibs' play could not be faulted on the count of lack of endeavour but there was about them a halting, unconvincing movement.' Another new Sauzée signing, French defender Lilian Martin, had made his debut in this match but hadn't looked particularly impressive.

The supporters still hadn't deserted Hibs or Franck Sauzée. Despite this being the club's eighteenth consecutive league match without a win, a crowd of just under 10,000 had turned up. A photograph of Sauzée on the touchline, taken during this match, shows the great man looking handsome, dignified, deeply thoughtful and, it cannot be denied, somewhat sad.

Matters had now reached crisis point. Hibs sat in second bottom position in the SPL. They were nine points ahead of St Johnstone and due to meet the Perth club the following week. A victory would stretch the gap between the two clubs and ease Hibs' relegation worries considerably. If, on the other hand, the unthinkable happened and St Johnstone won, then there would only be six points between the two teams and Hibs would be in very serious trouble indeed.

Most Hibs fans were of the opinion that their team would survive. They were aware that Franck Sauzée was not finding the transition from player to manager an easy one to make. They didn't, though, seriously expect to see Sauzée leaving his post this early in his managerial reign. By sheer coincidence, the list of pop charts in the Hibs' programme for the game against Dunfermline, just as it had done for the previous match with Celtic, had a definite resonance with the plight of the club's manager. Ten years ago, the second best-selling single in the country had been 'Stay' by Shakespeare's Sister. That would almost certainly have been the message that the Hibs support wanted to relay to Franck Sauzée.

However, the club's board of directors wasn't quite so sure. They were worried that the team was in freefall. It was over three months since a league victory had been recorded and the effect of a second relegation in four years would be catastrophic in financial terms. The board had also been concerned about the defeated look their manager had worn in the technical area during the League Cup semi-final defeat to Ayr. They wondered whether the job of football manager, which required a hard-edged, ruthless approach, was proving too much for an amiable, cultured man like Franck Sauzée.

The board was also acutely aware that, after a 2–2 draw with Hearts on New Year's Day 1998, then manager Jim Duffy had been given a stay of execution. When Duffy was eventually replaced by Alex McLeish, the few extra weeks in post that McLeish had lost out on through the club's delaying Duffy's departure proved crucial. McLeish had simply run out of games in his valiant attempt to keep the club in the top league. Now, the Hibs board was anxious to avoid such a thing happening again.

Lengthy meetings took place and the midnight oil was burned in the Easter Road boardroom. Finally, a decision was taken with the heaviest of hearts. On Wednesday, 20 February 2002, Rod Petrie and Malcolm McPherson visited Franck Sauzée at his New Town apartment. With great sadness, they informed Sauzée that his reign as manager of Hibernian Football Club, which had begun only sixty-nine days earlier, was about to come to an end.

Looking back on that melancholy night, Malcolm McPherson recalls the occasion with clarity. 'It was the most difficult thing I have ever done in my life,' he says.

'Franck was his usual courteous self. He accepted our news with great dignity and total equanimity. If I am being honest, I think that he appeared relieved that we had taken the decision. It was as if a weight had been removed from his shoulders.

'I remember Franck saying to us, "They didn't want a manager who talked to them and tried to understand them. They wanted someone who banged the table and shouted, 'F***! F***! F***!'" I got the impression that Franck just could not understand how some of his players could be weak mentally and settle for second best. He himself had always had great mental strength.'

Petrie and McPherson told Sauzée that the news would be made public the following day. They said that they would be holding a press conference and Franck intimated that he would like to be present at this event. It was agreed that this would happen.

Thus did realism intervene in the romance between Franck Sauzée and Hibernian Football Club. To this day, debate continues across the Hibernian community on whether or not the board's decision to dispense with Franck Sauzée's services so prematurely was justified.

The majority of fans would still argue that it wasn't. They would claim that Hibs had a squad of players who were simply too good to go down. This may well have been the case but despite numbering players of the quality of De la Cruz, Laursen, Brebner, Jack, O'Neil, Murray, Luna, Brewster and Zitelli in their ranks, Hibs were struggling badly.

It is difficult to explain why such a talented group of footballers was flirting with relegation. There had been a series of injuries to key players and some vital refereeing decisions had gone against Hibs, but neither of these incidences should have been sufficiently damaging to send the club so close to the bottom of the league.

Franck Sauzée had made a number of signings in Jarkko Wiss, Lilian Martin and Gary Caldwell, with Freddie Daquin lined up to follow. With the exception of the young Caldwell, who was only on a short-term loan, none of these players appeared likely to arrest Hibs' slide. Nor did Sauzée's record as manager of six draws, eight defeats and one solitary victory in fifteen matches make pleasant reading. However, it is undeniably true that no manager can be definitively judged on a three-month reign that spanned no more than fifteen games. This is not adequate time to succeed or fail.

The biggest contributory factor in Franck Sauzée's demise was, without doubt, his decision to stop playing. Already, without the highly talented Russell Latapy, Hibs had struggled in season 2001–2002 every time Franck Sauzée had been injured. When Sauzée played, Hibs rarely lost. When he was out of the side, they found it extremely difficult to win. By retiring from playing, Franck effectively deprived himself of the club's most accomplished defender and most creative influence in one fell swoop. The impact of this was that Gary Smith and Paul Fenwick, who had looked highly impressive with Sauzée behind them, looked less assured in his absence. The supply of high quality passes, which Sauzée had regularly provided for the Hibs front players, was also removed and this, too, had a significantly detrimental effect on the team.

Whatever the rights and wrongs of Sauzée's dismissal, there was bound to be a massive reaction when news of it reached the airwaves. So it proved. When Sky Sports News announced on their 'Breaking News' screen strap that Hibs had parted company with Franck Sauzée, the response was an amalgam of shock, dismay and anger that sent the radio phone-in programmes and fans' internet websites into meltdown.

The prevailing emotion, though, was sadness. There was universal agreement that it was tragic that a relationship between a French footballing superstar and an Edinburgh football club, which was so special that it could be genuinely termed unique, had ended in such a way. There was a real irony that a managerial reign that had started with such hope and optimism in a match against Dunfermline Athletic had come to an abrupt conclusion after another match against the same club less than ten short weeks later.

The news of Franck Sauzée's sacking had an impact of seismic proportions. The aftershocks are still being felt to this day.

13

THAT'S LIFE. THAT'S FOOTBALL.

WHEN MALCOLM McPherson and his fellow director Stephen Dunn met the press and media the next day to announce Sauzée's sacking, there is no doubt about who was perceived to be the villain of the piece. McPherson endured one of the most difficult experiences of his life. He recalls, 'No one admired Franck more than me. It was not a pleasant feeling to be sitting in a press conference knowing that I was being blamed for the fact that he was leaving Hibs. I understood why people felt as they did but I had acted in what I genuinely considered were the best interests of the club.'

When the directors finished answering questions, they moved aside and allowed Franck Sauzée the floor. McPherson recalls Franck's performance was impressive. 'He was elegant and eloquent in equal measure. There was a huge amount of goodwill towards him in the room.'

Suavely dressed in an expensively cut black suit and black polo neck jersey, Sauzée poured his heart out. He said, 'I have been wronged and I am hurt.' Franck was a proud man and had never known failure. What he perceived to be the premature termination of his spell as manager had clearly wounded him deeply.

Sauzée ended the press conference by repeating what had become his catch phrase as results and luck had continued to go against him during his tenure of the managerial hot seat. He philosophically declared: 'That's life. That's football.'

The reporting in the following day's newspapers was massively supportive of Franck Sauzée. Stuart Bathgate in *The Scotsman* described 'a funereal air at Easter Road'. The staff, he said, 'were genuinely shocked and saddened by Sauzée's untimely departure'. He added, 'There had been a death in the family all right.'

Remarking on how Sauzée had been forced to come to terms with the loss of Hibs' two best players in himself and Latapy, Bathgate went on to say, 'It doesn't matter if you are Fabio Capello, Héctor Cúper or any other coaching mastermind, you cannot overcome such problems in a matter of months.' He did add, though, 'And Franck is clearly no Capello or Cúper.'

In a well balanced piece, Bathgate gave Hibs credit for going for a 'cool Frenchman rather than a downmarket Scot' but took the club to task for not giving Sauzée the time he required to do his job successfully.

There was praise in the press for how Franck Sauzée had conducted himself in front of the media. Clearly upset, and indeed, close to tears at times, he had behaved in a dignified fashion, resisting the temptation to indulge in attacks on Hibs or wallow in self pity. He had left with his head held high. There was agreement, too, that Franck looked less stressed already than he had done in the latter days of his spell as manager.

Most supporters and almost all members of the media may have been of the opinion that the Hibs board had acted in haste and in error in dispensing with Sauzée's services after less than ten weeks in post, but there was general acknowledgement that Hibs had been honest and transparent in explaining their decisions.

The Hibs board took the view that in appointing Franck Sauzée, the club had been idealistic rather than realistic. There had proved to be a gap between Sauzée's character and the demands of managing a Scottish football team.

Franck had found it difficult to motivate some players who, unlike him, could not motivate themselves. He had tried to deal in his own pleasant, positive way with men who were used to being ruled by fear. There was no doubt that there would be much less charm and intelligence around Easter Road than had been the case during Franck Sauzée's time at Hibs, but the overriding fear of those in control of the club had been that Hibs would suffer a financially crippling second spell in the First Division in four years, unless they replaced Sauzée with a more pragmatic manager.

When Franck Sauzée walked out of Easter Road, a large part of the heart of the club went with him. Here was a footballer of the highest international calibre who had chosen to come to Edinburgh – not just to finish off his career quietly and pick up some money along the way. Sauzée had bought totally into the ethos of Hibernian Football Club. He had brought class and quality back to Easter Road and had literally shed blood on Hibs' behalf. Most of all, he had fallen in love with the club and its supporters and that feeling had been unreservedly reciprocated. In the aftermath of Sauzée's departure, Malcolm McPherson received a barrage of e-mails and letters. As the chairman himself puts it: 'Few of them were complimentary or began with a cordial "Dear Malcolm".'

To his credit, McPherson personally replied to all of the 1,400 or so messages that he received, with the exception of those that were downright abusive. There was no credit coming McPherson's way, though, from *The Scotsman* columnist and well known Hibs supporter, Aidan Smith. Hibs' board declared Smith was 'spineless'.

That is a moot point. It is unarguable that the board didn't give Franck Sauzée much time. It can also be argued, however, that knowing the amount of opprobrium that was bound to come down on their heads after taking their contentious decision, the directors displayed courage in biting the bullet rather than taking the easier option of leaving Franck in post and waiting to see how things panned out.

The object of the exercise had been to ensure Hibs' survival in the SPL. The club's next match was against St Johnstone, who sat just nine points below them in the league table. By the time this game came round, Bobby Williamson had been installed as the new manager of Hibs. Williamson had been highly successful during his spell in charge of Kilmarnock and it was hoped that his more prosaic approach to the game would enable Hibs to bring about an immediate reversal in their recent fortunes.

Hibs went in to the St Johnstone match on the back of a run of extremely poor form. They hadn't managed to win any of their last eighteen league games and had taken only eight points from a possible fifty-four. A crowd of 13,731 turned out for the game, which suggests that Hibs supporters realised how serious their team's plight was and were, despite their disenchantment at losing their most iconic player, prepared to support the club in its hour of need.

As it happened, Hibs won and won well. Two goals from young Ian Murray and a pile driver from Garry O'Connor secured a comfortable 3–0 victory.

All of a sudden, the gap between Hibs and Saints was twelve points. Another 3–0 victory at Livingston the following week placed Hibs fifteen points in front of St Johnstone and pretty much removed the threat of relegation.

These events can be looked at in two ways. There are those who will say that the board had panicked and that if they had stood by Franck Sauzée, the same victories and Hibs SPL safety would have been secured. Others would assert that defeat to St Johnstone would have seen a team in freefall find itself only six points clear of the bottom of the league with relegation a very real possibility.

Nick Colgan has no doubt where he stands on this issue. He says, 'We would definitely have beaten St Johnstone if Franck had still been in charge. That result had nothing to do with a change of manager and everything to do with a change of luck. Franck did not get a single scrap of luck in all his time in charge. Given time, I think that Franck would have made a fabulous manager. His appointment was popular with the fans but it was even more popular with the players.

'We were desperate for Franck to succeed. We couldn't have tried any harder. If anything, we tried too hard. Franck had a wonderful manner with the players and he knew the game inside out. It was a tragedy that he didn't get the time to finish the job which he had started.'

If the Hibs board had dismissed Franck Sauzée to ensure that their club remained in the top flight of Scottish football, then the first two results of Bobby Williamson's managerial reign very quickly achieved that aim. There are those to this day, however, who are convinced that the same results would have been attained if Franck Sauzée had remained in charge.

It is interesting to contemplate what might have happened if Franck Sauzée had remained in post. Bobby Williamson's reign saw a period of austerity ushered in at Easter Road. The kind of finance, based on significant income from Sky Television, that had been provided for Alex McLeish was no longer available. Williamson was forced to make do and mend. He was less than entirely successful in doing so. Malcolm McPherson, while understanding the need for increased economy, considered that the club was being overly stringent and losing its ambition in the process. He resigned as chairman of Hibs. It is highly unlikely that Franck Sauzée, if he had kept his job, would have relished the task of attempting to take Hibs forward in straitened circumstances.

Interestingly, Malcolm McPherson now considers that his colleagues on the board were correct to take the steps they did. He says, 'The action Rod Petrie and the other directors advocated at the time has been proved to be the correct way forward. The club wouldn't be as financially healthy as it is now if they had continued to spend money as freely as before.'

Before Sauzée returned to France, he made one last visit to Easter Road. The Franck Sauzée Appreciation Society had organised a function to pay tribute to Franck and make a presentation to him before he went home. A capacity audience composed of both committed celebrity supporters, like Irvine Welsh and Dougray Scott, and ordinary dyed-in-the-wool Hibs fans joined the great man for the most emotional of occasions. Franck made time for everyone. Photographs were taken, autographs signed and tears shed. Sauzée himself made an outstanding and poignant speech.

Even when Franck was back on French soil, the affair rumbled on. There were differences between Hibs and Franck's representatives over the amount of compensation that he was due. All was not sweetness and light and, for a time, it seemed like matters might need to be resolved in the Court of Session. Happily, agreement between the two parties was reached and Sauzée received the 'handsome settlement' that most people considered to be his due.

When interviewed a year later, Franck was living quietly back in France. He told his interviewer that he was indulging in a process of 'regeneration'. In other words, he was taking time to find himself again.

So ended a significant era in Hibs history. Franck Sauzée had arrived at Hibs in February 1999. Just over three years later, it was time for him to depart. He left behind him memories of that rare combination of qualities – a high class footballer who was also a great man. Quite some time has elapsed since Franck Sauzée's departure from Hibs. In the years that have passed since his going, he is still spoken about in the Hibernian Family in tones of reverence and deep affection. That is simply because, to Hibs fans, he became 'one of their own'. That status will never change. Franck Sauzée was, is and always will be a true Hibernian Hero.

14

FRANCK SAUZÉE, HIBERNIAN HERO

IN THIS chapter, a range of football people take the opportunity to share their memories of Franck Sauzée. They include managers, directors, journalists, broadcasters and players. They all have their own special recollections of Le God.

Alex McLeish, of course, was the manager who identified Franck Sauzée as his 'marquee signing'. He had the confidence and courage to believe that he could talk Sauzée into joining a Scottish First Division team, as well as the standing in the game and powers of persuasion to enable him to convince Sauzée that not only would he be good for Hibs but also that Hibs would be good for him. McLeish was to be proved emphatically correct on both scores.

Here is how Alex McLeish remembers Franck Sauzée: 'Franck Sauzée was the best player I ever worked with, with the ball at his feet. He had a phenomenal range of passing. I always thought that he was a similar player to the Dutchman, Ronald Koeman. Franck was a naturally laid back man but there was something special about him that inspired other players. They looked at him and thought if Franck can do that, so can we.

'As a manager, it is important to be your own man. I have taken bits from Alex Ferguson and Jock Stein but mostly I am myself. I always wanted my players to have strong mentalities. Franck had a very strong mind.'

John Hughes was Franck Sauzée's predecessor as captain of Hibs. The brash Leither and the cultured Frenchman were different people but got on very well. Sauzée really admired Yogi's motivational powers. Indeed, he gave his skipper huge credit for putting the Hibs team in the right frame of mind for the Millennium Derby victory over Hearts in December 1999.

Listen to Hughes' view of his former colleague: 'Franck was a big-game player. He knew how to turn it on when it really mattered. You would have trouble getting the ball off Franck in a telephone box. He was a gentleman, too – a real humble guy for such a great player. By the time Franck came to Hibs, his legs weren't so sharp but his brain was sharper than ever. He knew where the ball was going before it arrived.'

Russell Latapy joined forces with Franck Sauzée in giving Hibs back their pride and their proper position in Scottish football. Russell rarely wasted a ball and he wasn't one for wasting words either. When he and Sauzée were causing problems for SPL teams on a weekly basis, the Little Magician simply said, 'Franck has class. Rangers and Celtic would love to have him.'

One of the Old Firm giants did, of course, lure Latapy away from Easter Road. It would have been interesting to see what would have happened had either of Scotland's Big Two pursued an interest in Franck Sauzée. All Hibs fans would like to think that Franck would have stayed at Easter Road.

The *Edinburgh Evening News* Hibs correspondent David Hardie has followed and written about the club's fortunes for many years now. He was very close to the action when Franck Sauzée played for and managed Hibs and his views are all the more valuable for that reason.

Here is how David recalls Sauzée: 'Franck was a courteous, cultured, charming, intelligent, modest man. He loved living in Edinburgh. He was certainly no Big Time Charlie. Franck wasn't just good for Hibs, he was good for Scottish football. I can't think of any other Hibs player receiving a standing ovation from the Celtic fans at Parkhead, as Franck did.'

Hardie went on, 'As a player, Franck was classy but hard when he had to be. All top players have a ruthless streak in them and Franck was no exception. I remember him telling me that the great Marseille team he played for used to keep their opponents waiting in the tunnel before the game. When they eventually arrived, they would eyeball them. For the first fifteen minutes of the match, Marseille would hammer their opponents and, only when they had asserted their mental and physical authority, would they open out and start to play their football.

'Once, when we were on a family holiday in Provence, my daughter was wearing her Hibs strip. Lots of French people kept coming up to us, pointing at her and saying, "Ah Sauzée!" Another time in Provence, we went into a golf club at a course which had been designed by Seve Ballesteros. In the foyer, there was a huge photograph of Franck playing golf. Above the photo, there was a caption, which read, "A Sauzée Master Class". Franck was a tremendous player. He could ping fifty- or sixty-yard passes straight to feet.'

Another media man who thinks highly of Sauzée is the doyen of Scottish sports reporters, Chick Young. Chick's thoughts on the great man make interesting reading.

'There are players who waft through the Scottish game like a dream in the night. You look back thinking: "Did that really happen?"

'Me? I get wistful at the mention of John White, an Alloa, Falkirk, Tottenham Hotspur and Scotland inside right. If you don't know what an inside right is, ask your dad, or granddad more probably. John – "The Ghost of White Hart Lane" they called him – was killed by lightning on a golf course when he was just twenty-four and given the limited television coverage of football in the sixties, which in any case happened in grainy black and white, I really couldn't have seen that much of him. But to this day, I recall always pretending to be him in the school playground. And the number 8 jersey will be forever mine in any kickabout.

'Sauzée's like that. "Le God" they called Franck. Was it too much bother to look up the French for God? But he was a mesmerising talent. And a lovely fella.

'There is a standing joke on our BBC Scotland *Sportsound* programme which insists I usually have my player of the year nominated before the Christmas lights come down. But in – I think – 1999 or 2000, I surpassed myself. I was punting Franck for the title before the autumn leaves were down.

'He was fantastic. Easter Road had become football's pleasure dome and the Frenchman was its ringmaster.

'I saw Brownlie and Blackley and Stanton and Best in Hibernian jerseys but Sauzée was peerless.

'It was as if he had a GPS view of the game, a pinpoint knowledge of where every player was at every phase of play. And the wherewithal to pick out those with whom he shared a dressing room with a miraculous pass. Maybe it's my mind playing tricks, but I don't even recall him breaking sweat doing it. Sauzée could have played in his suit and brogues.

'He was a top bloke, too. He played at Marseille, a club whose home is in my favourite part of France. I fell in love with Provence a long time ago and I used to love talking to Franck about life there. It's like Leith, only more beautiful.

'Great players are those who, if you were a fan of no club in particular, would make you pay your money on a Saturday just to watch them play. They are few and far between. But Franck Sauzée, at the turn of the century, made the journey east from Glasgow along the damned M8 – maybe the most boring road in Europe – a pleasure because the sense of anticipation ate the miles.

'By heaven, he was good. The Dear Lord only knows how good he was. Le God, Le best.'

Chick's *Sportsound* colleague, the urbane Richard Gordon, who does such a superb job of orchestrating the programme, also has a high opinion of Monsieur Sauzée. The praise that is forthcoming from such an authority on the Scottish game speaks volumes for the impression made by Franck during his time in Scotland. Here are Richard's thoughts:

'Having watched Franck Sauzée orchestrate the Marseille side that lifted the first ever Champions League in 1992–93, I was intrigued when I heard that Alex McLeish had somehow enticed him to the Scottish First Division. I feared that it was another case of an ailing old pro looking for one last pay day, but I should have known better.

'From the moment he arrived at Easter Road, Franck captured the hearts of the Hibernian fans and illuminated the Scottish game in general. He had that Gallic arrogance so common to many of his countrymen, but never in an overbearing way. It was an arrogance borne out of the self belief, the certain knowledge that he was better than most, if not all, of the other players on the park. I loved to watch him stroke passes around the pitch, only rarely failing to connect with a team mate, while at the same time directing those around him. His football vision was finely tuned, he always seemed to be a move or two ahead of both his colleagues and opponents. He was on the whole a joy to watch, a player who left an indelible mark on our game.

'The big disappointment was, of course, that he somehow failed to adapt his many talents to the role of management, or at least during the short time afforded him by the Easter Road board of directors. It was a crying shame that he left the club in the way he did, but his memory remains unsullied, his legacy still rightly celebrated by Hibees everywhere.

'Quite apart from his on-field mastery, my abiding memory of Franck is that he was an all-round decent guy, a man who charmed with his smile and the intelligence of his conversation. He richly deserves to be remembered as a true Hibernian great.'

Radio Forth DJ, former *Scotsport* host, pantomime star, Hibs corporate hospitality compere and *Edinburgh Evening News* columnist Grant Stott, is, like his father and brother, a dyed-in-the-wool Hibee. Grant is in no doubt about how much Franck Sauzée meant, and continues to mean, to Hibs fans. His comments on the great man will strike a chord with every Hibs supporter.

'Over the years, every now and then, usually within each generation of Hibs fans, a special player adorns the green and white of Hibs and becomes a hero to a legion of fans. A player so special, that the mere mention of his name can result in an instant, knowing smile across the face of any Hibs fan who was lucky enough to see him play, usually accompanied by the phrase "oh, what a player he was".'

'In my Dad's case, it was Joe Baker. Before him, you could choose between Gordon Smith or Lawrie Reilly (or any of the Famous Five for that matter). Pat Stanton arrived in the sixties and graced the pitch along with the likes of Peter Cormack, Jimmy O'Rourke and Alan Gordon to name just a few, but each taking a special place in many fans' hearts. No one could believe it when George Best arrived and although he was past his glory days, was still able to turn it on when he was in the mood.'

'But for me, the player who without a doubt achieved that Le God-like status amongst myself and other fans like me, was Franck Sauzée. Like the day George Best signed, there was a sense of disbelief when Franck arrived at Hibs. Disbelief that we had secured the services of such a player and that, also like George, his best days were perhaps behind him. But no. He not only influenced those who sat agog watching him in the stands, but those who played around him.'

'It was like Hibs was his destiny; such was the relationship he had with the Club and the fans. A true legend in the history of Hibernian Football Club and my one wish is that one day he gets the send-off from the fans that he deserves.

'Franck Sauzée. Oh what a player he was.'

Yet another broadcaster with a positive perspective on the Aubenas Aristocrat is Sky Sports reporter Luke Shanley. Luke states, 'I was too young to see the Famous Five, Joe Baker or Pat Stanton so Franck Sauzée is undoubtedly the best Hibs player I have ever seen in the flesh.

'I was in sixth year at school when Franck got sacked as manager. It was during the February mid-term holiday so I made my way to

Easter Road from my house as soon as I heard the news. I arrived just as Franck was leaving the ground. I shook his hand and wished him well. I thought that that would be the last time I would ever see Franck but in 2008 I was covering a Rangers v Fiorentina UEFA Cup semi-final match at Ibrox for the now defunct Talk 107 radio station. Sitting below me in the media area was none other than Franck Sauzée, who was covering the game for French TV. At half time, I went down and spoke to Franck and he couldn't have been more pleasant.

'My biggest claim to fame on the Sauzée front, though, is that I have his overcoat/jacket that he used to wear on the touchline when he was manager. My friend's dad was a teacher at Preston Lodge secondary school in East Lothian and his dad's friend, Jim Anderson, a French teacher at the school, was teaching Franck and David Zitelli English in his spare time. When Franck left Hibs, he gave the coat to Jim. Jim passed it on to my friend and he very kindly passed it on to me. As a dedicated collector of all things Hibernian, I was delighted to get it and best of all, it even fits me not too badly.'

Journalist, broadcaster and author of that splendid Hibs book *Sunshine on Leith*, Simon Pia also has Sauzée memories to share. Here are Simon's recollections: 'I remember Franck's debut at Brockville and it really gave no inkling of what lay ahead for both him and Hibs.

'Here he was, a guy with a Champions League medal, on a bleak day in Falkirk, shoulders hunched against the cold. He spent most of the match rubbing his hands as the ball whizzed over his head from end to end on that tight wee pitch. He must have wondered what he had let himself in for.

'But from that inauspicious start, it turned out all so differently for Franck, Hibs and Scottish football. He went on to become Stanton-esque – no greater compliment – directing Hibs from the back. Alex McLeish moved him to sweeper after a spell in midfield and it worked a treat. He was the best in the league by a kilometre.

'The only time I ever saw him in trouble was once against Henrik Larsson, but Henrik was in his prime and Franck's legs had slowed down a bit. But class never dies. Two big moments stand out and will never go away, both of them against Hearts. His goal in the Millennium Derby and the day he lost four front teeth for the Hibees. They even made a song about it. A pop duo called Masters of Truemanship released a single in 2004 with two Sauzée themed mixes – *The Man from Marseille* and *4 Front Teeth*.

'Franck told me later it was Yogi who had whipped them up on the bus on the way to Tynecastle for the Millennium Derby in December 1999. I even hugged John Gibson in the press box that night as Franck smashed in the second. I'd like to stress it is the one and only time I've kissed John. Franck's header when he lost his teeth epitomised the man – skill, athleticism and raw courage as he got up, stuffed gauze in his bloody mouth and played on.

'It was probably only Alex McLeish who could have got him to Hibs. Andy Roxburgh said whenever Scotland went abroad, the player everyone knew was big Alex. He had that charisma. They'd played against each other as international adversaries and Alex also had a European medal. Merci, Alex and merci, Franck.'

Malcolm McPherson was on the Hibs board of directors when Franck Sauzée signed for the club. He was chairman at Easter Road when Sauzée was appointed manager and then dismissed from his post. McPherson's admiration for Sauzée is unreserved. 'Franck was the same on and off the park. He was elegant, sophisticated, suave and intelligent. He was a charismatic man who was quintessentially French. He was an absolute gentleman and used to attend dinner parties with the New Town glitterati and mix with the cream of Edinburgh society.

'He had played at a higher standard than those he played with and against in Scotland and it showed. There was a definite aura about him. He went on the field expecting to win and that rubbed off on the other players.

'He liked the good things in life like fine French wine. There is a story, probably not true, which did the rounds during Franck's time at Hibs. He used to receive deliveries of top quality red wine from his wine merchant in France. One day he brought a bottle of this wine into the dressing room to share with his team mates. Franck opened the bottle and laid it on the table. He then went to get some glasses. When he came back in, John Hughes was glugging the wine from the bottle. Yogi said, "Hey Franck, this wine's good stuff." Only Yogi himself could tell you if that really happened or if it was just a good story. I suspect it was the latter.'

Lawrie Reilly, the goal-scoring machine who spearheaded Hibs' Famous Five forward line, got to know Franck Sauzée during the Frenchman's time with Hibs. Lawrie takes a bit of convincing that most modern players are as good as the greats whom he played alongside but, where Franck Sauzée was concerned, he had no doubts whatsoever. Lawrie says, 'Franck would have definitely got into the Famous Five team but I am not prepared to say whose place he would have taken. He was a true gentleman. My wife Iris and I met him once at a function at Easter Road. A couple of days later, we met Franck, his wife and his parents in John Lewis. Iris mentioned the social event we had been at. "Ah oui," said Franck, "of course, the soiree!"'

Many Hibs fans saw great similarities between Franck Sauzée and the one and only Pat Stanton. They were both equally happy in defence or midfield, classy players but not without a bit of steel, always had time on the ball and never wasted possession and both provided a significant goal threat to the teams they came up against. Pat has no reservations whatsoever in expressing his admiration for Franck.

'Franck had an aura of greatness about him. He read the game brilliantly and used the ball superbly. Franck's searching passes took his team mates into positions that they might never have gone into of their own accord. He was the perfect example to any young player.

'Franck could have come to Hibs and big-timed it but he didn't because he wasn't that sort of man. He bought completely into Hibs as a club. That is why the supporters loved him so much.

'That and his immense talent as a footballer. The biggest difficulty Franck faced as a manager was that he couldn't pick himself. When Franck stopped playing, the heart and a lot of the quality went out of the Hibs team. I picked Franck for my Hibernian Dream Team and that tells you just how highly I rate him. He definitely belongs in the top echelon of Hibs players.'

Currently in his testimonial year, Ian Murray has been an outstanding servant to Hibs. Ian has had the distinction of both playing with Franck Sauzée and being managed by him. Ian thinks the world of Sauzée. 'The first thing which struck me about Franck when he came to Hibs was that he had very little interest in material things. He must have been very well off but you would never have known it. He never boasted about his wealth or flaunted what he had. Money and possessions didn't seem important to him. Winning football matches most certainly did.

'As a player, he was great to play with. He would tell you what to do on the park but he wasn't a shouter. He was just like a manager on the pitch. He had a natural authority about him and I learned a lot just by watching Franck during a game. For all his great skill, he was a hard player as well and he could certainly take the knocks.

'Because of his reputation and his influence on Hibs' play, other teams used to target Franck. You would have had to have seen the bruises on his legs after a game to believe them. He took a lot of punishment. He never complained though. All the players got on well with Franck during his time at Easter Road. He would join us on our nights out but he never drank more than one glass of red wine.

'When I think of Franck at Hibs, I always think of his combination with Russell Latapy. They were a fantastic combination on the park but like chalk and cheese off it. Russell trained hard but he also partied hard. Franck had a more rigorous life style. Russell had tremendous individual skills but Franck was the better all round player. Together, they brought class to Hibs.'

Stuart Lovell was also a team mate of Franck Sauzée during the great man's time at Easter Road. Stuart is full of praise for Franck. 'When you think of his phenomenal footballing CV, Franck Sauzée was an incredibly humble man. There was no arrogance about him at all. What he did have was a tremendous presence. He was also physically imposing. Most of all, though, he had huge self belief. No player, team or game ever worried Franck. He went into every match knowing he was better than the opposition and expecting to win, and this definitely rubbed off on the rest of us.

'They say that when you meet your heroes, you can be disappointed. If any Hibs fan had met Franck, the opposite would have been true. It would be difficult to find a nicer man.'

Stuart also rates Sauzée highly as a player. 'Franck could do anything with the ball. He was as good a passer as I have ever seen. I include all the players I played with and against in my career and all those playing today in that statement. He really was that good. The young lads at the club used to watch him play in practice games and marvel at his ability. They couldn't believe some of the passes he used to make.'

Franck's shooting impressed Lovell, too. 'I remember a few of us used to do a bit of extra finishing practice after training on a Friday. Nick Colgan would go in goal and you would play the ball to a colleague who would lay it off for you to take a first time shot from the eighteen-yard line.

'It helped Nick sharpen his reflexes and he was hard to beat. If you managed to score with around half of your finishes, you were quite pleased. One day Franck decided to join in. He asked the rest of us to nominate where he should put the ball. It didn't matter where we specified he should place the ball, bottom right-hand corner, top left-hand corner or wherever, he curled it in perfectly each time. His shots all combined power, pace and precision. It was a masterly exhibition. After Franck had scored nine times in a row, Nick suggested that enough was enough. I won't tell you exactly what he said, but the gist of it was that he didn't take kindly to being shown up and he would prefer it if Franck didn't join in on future Fridays.'

Sauzée had class off the field as well as on it as Lovell recalls. 'I remember discussing wine with Franck. I was putting the case for

New World wines, which were starting to sell really well at that time. Franck, of course, was singing the praises of French wine. Next day, he brought me in a bottle of French red. He handed it to me with a smile and simply said, "It is good. Please don't waste it." I looked the wine up and it cost £50 a bottle. When I tasted it, its quality matched its price range. That was Franck, generous and classy, and an all round top man.

'Looking back now, I wonder about Franck's appointment as manager. At the time, there was a clamour from the fans for Franck to get the job and it seemed like a really good move when he was installed as Hibs boss. On reflection, I think Franck himself may have had doubts if the timing was right for him but, as always, he did what he thought the club and the fans wanted. He put Hibs first. Sometimes when players go back to their old clubs as manager and things don't work out, it can sully their reputation in the eyes of the supporters. Graeme Souness at Liverpool is a case in point. There is no doubt that he is less highly thought of by their fans now than he was before he became manager. Thankfully, that is not the case with Franck. His stint in the manager's chair did not affect his popularity with the Hibs support at all. The fans still love him and that is important.'

One of Stuart's former colleagues, John O'Neil, also has nothing but complimentary words for Franck Sauzée. John says, 'Everyone at Easter Road regarded Franck very highly as a player and a man. I certainly did.

'For such an outstanding footballer with so many great achievements behind him, he was a great person. Franck was a modest man who was private and didn't seek the limelight. He was happier to see his team mates get the credit.

'As a player, he had tremendous touch and that created time and space for him. Nick Colgan, our goalkeeper, hardly kicked the ball out. Nick would throw the ball to Franck, who would take it in really tight situations.

'You would be thinking, "Oh no, Nick, what have you done? He's got somebody closing in on him," but Franck would receive the ball, control it instantly, beat a man and start a move. He wasn't boastful but he had a strong self confidence and believed in his own ability. He really made things happen for Hibs from the back and was a joy to play with.'

Nick Colgan, himself, doesn't hide his admiration for Sauzée. Nick loved his time at Hibs and is always happy to reminisce about his days at Easter Road. He recalls, 'My time at Hibs was the highlight of my career. If I had had my way, I would never have left. What an honour it was to play with Franck Sauzée.

'People said that Franck's legs had gone by the time he came to Hibs. Take it from me, Franck didn't need speed with the talent he had. He had an incredible range of passing and would take the ball from a team mate at any time. As a goalkeeper, I knew that I could always throw the ball out to Franck and he would not only retain possession but set a move in motion.

'Franck was a pleasure to be around. He was a truly humble man and he wouldn't talk about all his great achievements in the game. He preferred to help the rest of us and he was a tremendous influence both on the field and in the dressing room. He was always approachable but what struck me most was the passion he brought to the game. He had a real winner's mentality and that rubbed off on the rest of us. His signing was a major coup by Alex McLeish.'

When Keith Wright joined Hibs in 1991, he had an immediate galvanising effect on the club. The team's form improved and they won the Skol League Cup within months of Keith's arrival. The man himself scored in every round of the competition, of course, and notched the decisive second goal in the final. Keith considers that Franck Sauzée coming to Hibs also had a positive impact in helping the club to move forward in a big way, as he explains.

'Franck came to the club when things were quite low after relegation the season before. He gave everyone a massive lift with not only his performances but his presence on and off the field. I knew Paul Fenwick well from my time at Morton and he always told me how his game and other players' were improved so much after playing alongside Franck.

'Franck's touch, vision and passing range were top notch and I often wondered what he would have been like at the peak of his career. I and most Hibees will remember Franck for the derbies. His performance in the 6–2 derby was unbelievable.

'As a Hibs fan growing up, I had a group of players that made me proud to support Hibs and they were all players I had read about or watched before I played for Hibs. These included the Famous Five, Pat Stanton, Jimmy O'Rourke, Ally MacLeod, Alex Edwards, Des Bremner, Alex Cropley, John Brownlie, John Blackley and Jackie McNamara. Frank Sauzée is now part of that group and, in my opinion, would have fitted in perfectly to the Turnbull's Tornadoes team! I would have loved to play with Franck.'

Keith's friend and colleague Mickey Weir is equally enthusiastic about Franck Sauzée's impact on Hibs. Mickey was delighted when Hibs signed Franck. 'I always think that Hibs and their fans deserve the best and I knew that that was exactly what they were getting when they signed Franck Sauzée. It was obvious that he had both experience and class. Watching him play as an older player, you could tell just how good he must have been when he was at his peak.

'When I was under-21 coach at Motherwell, Billy Davies, who was manager at Fir Park at that time, sent me to watch Hibs as Motherwell were due to play them in a couple of weeks' time. Franck was playing sweeper by then and he orchestrated everything that Hibs did. Even though he was often receiving the ball on his own eighteen-yard line, he still posed a real threat to other teams as he would open them up with a forty- or fifty-yard pinpoint pass. I put all this in my report to Billy. I know that he hatched a plan to keep Franck quiet but I don't think it totally worked. When the game came round, Franck still exerted a big influence on it. He was just too good a player to be nullified.'

Another Hibs star from the Alex Miller era is Darren Jackson. Darren didn't have the privilege of playing with Franck Sauzée but he did play against him. Darren remembers, 'I first came up against Franck in a derby match. I had moved from Celtic to Hearts by then and it was my first game at Easter Road in a maroon jersey. I think it's fair to say that the Hibs fans weren't slow to let me know that they weren't too impressed by my switch of loyalties. That was bad enough but then Franck Sauzée got me booked. I tackled him and he went down as though I had committed an assault on him. Stuart Dougal was the referee and he wasted no time in flashing a yellow card at me. I couldn't believe it. That was the old pro in Franck but it didn't take me long to realise that he had a lot more to offer than experience.

'I played against Franck when he was in midfield and also when he had moved back to sweeper. He was magnificent in both positions. I played with some great players – Paul Gascoigne and Peter Beardsley at Newcastle and Henrik Larsson, Lubo Moravcik and Paolo Di Canio at Celtic. I also played against some of the top players in the world in my Scotland days and Franck was right up there with the very best of them.

'He was also a really nice man. For somebody who had achieved so much in the game, he was very modest. There wasn't a hint of arrogance about him. He treated all players the same whether they were top stars like himself or Third Division players. He was natural and pleasant with everyone. That was Franck Sauzée, totally classy both on and off the park.'

The Hibernian Former Players Association, which is chaired by Paul Kane, does much good work for charitable causes and also recognises the contribution that past players have made to the club. Paul was happy to put a discussion of Franck Sauzée's impact at Easter Road on the agenda at one of the association's meetings. There was unanimity that Sauzée had brought quality and leadership. Those players who had played with Jackie McNamara recalled how Jackie had organised them on the field and had always gone out of his way to support and encourage his team mates off the pitch, too. They felt that Franck Sauzée had had exactly the same influence on his colleagues in the Hibs side during his time with the club.

Kenny Davidson, the skilful winger who played during Eddie Turnbull's early days as manager, summed up the difference

Sauzée made as follows: 'Franck Sauzée took Hibs on to a new level when he arrived,' said Kenny. 'It's as simple as that.'

The words of these football men speak for themselves. They all hold Franck Sauzée in high esteem as a football player and as a man.

There is another group that reveres the great man and that, of course, is the Hibernian support. The next chapter provides these faithful followers of the Leith team with the opportunity to pay tribute to the man they christened Le God.

15

THE FANS REMEMBER FRANCK

HIBS SUPPORTERS don't expect constant success. They accept inconsistency because they are used to it and continue to turn up even when their team is in the doldrums. They have known halcyon days, though, and they always crave for a return to the best of times. Every so often their wish is fulfilled and they are able to watch high quality players in the green and white as the team challenges for honours. This was the situation when Alex McLeish was in charge at Easter Road. McLeish transformed the team, provided weekly entertainment for the fans and raised expectations in the East of Edinburgh.

A major reason for Big Alex's success was the signing of two players of the highest class in Russell Latapy and Franck Sauzée. Hibees loved Latapy and admired his silky skills. They enjoyed them while they could because they always suspected that Hibs would be a stopping off point on his footballing journey, and so it proved.

Sauzée was different. Here was a true all-time footballing great who made it clear from the outset that he had fallen in love with Hibs and had no intention of leaving the club in a hurry. When he did depart, of course, he didn't do so of his own volition. The fans, for their part, wasted no time in taking Sauzée to their hearts. They knew that this man was special and that Alex McLeish had signed an iconic player. In the modern world, long-term commitment is a scarce commodity in football. Players come and go with bewildering rapidity yet, ironically, the term legend is bandied around casually and often without justification. The currency of legendary status has undoubtedly been devalued, so if someone makes an authentic claim to be described as a genuine legend then they have to be seen as a player of extraordinary gifts. Franck Sauzée meets this criterion with ease and does, indeed, merit the appellation of legend. What follows is a summary of the views of a cross section of supporters of Hibs on Franck and his time with the Hibees.

Best-selling Scottish novelist Irvine Welsh has never hidden his love of the Hibees. The club crops up regularly in his books and even though he has lived abroad a lot of the time in recent years, he has rarely been without a season ticket for Easter Road. Here is Welsh's take on Franck Sauzée's time at his beloved team.

'At Hibs, his legs may have been heavier than of old, but like all gifted footballers easing into the veteran years, he made up for this with his incredible vision and anticipation. Sauzée invariably sensed where the ball was going next and made everything look so easy. Instead of dictating from the midfield, he stepped back to do it from the sweeper's position, yet still loved to surge forward and was always a goal threat.

'Striding on to the park like a casual Colossus, his presence was simultaneously an inspiration and a calming influence on those around him, both on the field and in the stands. Some players often appear bigger than their chosen sport; they have a grace and presence which seems to throw aside the shackles of its limitations. Franck Sauzée possessed the bearing of a man who understood not just the beautiful game, but the world in general and his place in it.'

Derek Emslie is better known as Lord Kingarth, the QC and High Court judge. A fine sportsman himself, Derek played football for Spartans and rugby for Edinburgh Wanderers.

Indeed, while playing for Cambridge University against Oxford at the old Wembley, he became the first man to have his name appear on the electric scoreboard at the stadium. Derek is a lifelong

Hibs supporter and became a close friend of Franck Sauzée's during Franck's time at Hibs.

Derek recalls, 'Franck was a family man. He was devoted to his partner Guylaine and his daughters Estelle and Eloise. He loved living in Edinburgh. He was interested in art, food and wine. He also had a passion for fishing, which he indulged regularly. He truly loved Hibs and their fans, especially the passion they showed for the club. He loved to meet them in the street and talk about Hibs with them.

'Franck would come to our house for supper on a Sunday evening or we would go out for a meal to an Italian restaurant. He was always good company. He made time for everyone and made everyone feel important. My children Katie, Simon and Lucy are all great Hibs fans and, initially, they were a little bit in awe of Franck. He was so nice to them, though, always taking an interest in what they were doing, that they came to really enjoy his company.

'I remember once when Katie was going to a Halloween Fancy Dress party at Franck's house in the New Town. Franck's partner was there, too, as were David Zitelli and his wife. The taxi driver taking my daughter turned out to be a big Hibs fan. When he heard that Katie was going to Franck Sauzée's house, he said that he would go the door with her to try to catch a glimpse of the great man. Katie rang the bell. The door opened and a person in a monster costume picked her up and carried her upstairs to the sitting room. When he got into the room, the "monster" removed his fake head to reveal the smiling face of Franck Sauzée. Katie had to go back downstairs and reassure the taxi driver, who was looking a little worried, that it was only Franck having a laugh.

'As a player, Franck was magnificent. My dad was a Third Lanark fan who took me to Easter Road when I was young to see Falkirk playing Hibs. He was a great admirer of the Famous Five and he wanted me to see Gordon Smith and the rest of that great forward line in action. As soon as the Hibs team ran on to the field, I fell in love with their green and white strips and I have been a Hibs supporter ever since. Eddie Turnbull once told me that the Hibs strip is the "best kit there is" and he was right. Franck looked great in the Hibs strip. He had a real aura about him. Part of it was his sheer size!

'He was really good at making others play. He always made time for the younger players and brought out the best in players like Stuart Lovell. He felt that Lovell was underrated and thought he brought a lot to the Hibs team.

'Franck loved playing against Hearts and loved to beat them. He used to say, "Ah, ze derby." I always remember Franck sitting slumped over and dejected on the Hampden pitch after we lost the 2001 Scottish Cup Final to Celtic.

'He was desperate to win that cup for Hibs. If he had managed to do it, he would have considered it the greatest achievement of his career and that is really saying something.

'Every year, the Scottish judges hold a guest dinner. There are thirty-two of us and we all invite a guest who is not a member of the legal profession. One year I brought Franck along as my guest. He was resplendent in full Highland regalia and stole the show. Lord Kirkwood, who is a big Hearts supporter, said afterwards, "I have never met a nicer, more modest man."

'Even after he had lost his job as Hibs manager, Franck was kind enough to donate his Marseille French Championship winning jersey to a charity auction I was organising. I made sure that I was the highest bidder when that lot came up!

'I was a bit concerned when Franck phoned me from France and told me that he was possibly going to become Hibs manager after Alex McLeish had left. I was worried that it might be a little too soon for him. I think I would have preferred to have seen him start off as a coach working with somebody like Craig Brown before graduating to the role of manager.

'After Franck had been sacked, I went round to his house and we sat and talked for three hours. He was very hurt and very down. He had only ever known success in his life. He told me that he had a network of contacts in France who were identifying talented young players for him. He had planned to bring these players to

Hibs in the summer and was confident that he would have made Hibs successful. Sadly, neither Franck nor the Hibs support were given time to discover whether or not his feelings were accurate.

'Franck just did not see his sacking coming. He was totally taken aback. If Franck Sauzée came back to Easter Road, they could fill the ground without putting a match on.'

Another Hibs fan with interesting views on Franck Sauzée is Graeme Cadger. Graeme has been friendly with many Hibs players over the years. Indeed, he has helped some of them organise their testimonial matches and is currently the chairperson of Ian Murray's Testimonial Committee. Graeme also has a highly impressive collection of Hibernian memorabilia, including one of Franck Sauzée's French international jerseys. Here are Graeme's thoughts on the Le God: 'Franck was definitely not your stereotypical footballer. He had a really wide range of interests. Although he was modest and softly spoken, he very much knew his own worth. He was a private man yet he always made time for the fans. He understood what Hibs meant to the supporters. His presence on the field in a green and white strip lifted those around him. I always think of him as a great iconic French football figure at our club in the same way that Eric Cantona was at Manchester United.'

Willie McEwan is another well known Hibs fan who has been involved in a range of initiatives with the club and its players. Willie is in no doubt that Alex McLeish did excellent work when he persuaded Franck Sauzée to sign for Hibs. 'Franck's signing was exactly what Hibs needed at that time. The few months he spent in the First Division allowed him to attune himself to the Scottish game and he was able to hit the ground running when the team returned to the SPL.'

John Campbell has quite a Hibernian pedigree. He is a former editor of the fanzine *Hibs Monthly Mass Hibsteria*, has done important historical work for Hibs' official club website, has commentated for Hibernian TV, has contributed to Hibs match programmes and has recently written a trilogy that covers the club's fortunes since the end of World War Two. John has this to say about Franck Sauzée's time at Hibs: 'I'll be perfectly honest in saying that I didn't really know a lot about Franck Sauzée when I heard that Hibs had signed him and the few facts I did have pretty much failed to excite me. True, he had won medals at the highest level.

'However, his age and his willingness to come to the football backwaters of the Scottish League led to my first impressions being that he was looking for a nice easy way to wind down his career. After all, if he was still any good he wouldn't be coming anywhere near Easter Road would he?

'How wrong I was. From the first moment I saw him in the green and white of Hibernian I just knew he was a class act that would richly enhance our team and our club, and I will be forever grateful to Alex McLeish for persuading Le God to come here.

'My abiding memory of Franck was when I got the chance to interview him for the official Hibs website. I can tell you I was pretty nervous because my French is about as good as Del Boy Trotter's, but I needn't have worried as Franck proved to be a very calming influence on me and we got on like a house on fire.

'His obvious passion for "the Heebs" came shining through as he fielded each of my questions in a gentle and friendly manner and he surprised me somewhat in his knowledge of the history of the club, but that was soon explained when Franck told me that John Hughes had "impressed upon him" how important it was to beat Hearts and that Yogi's passion for Hibs encouraged him to find out all he could about our great club. In Franck's own words, which were spoken with a gleam in his eye as he surveyed his surroundings, "How could I turn down the chance to play for this great club?"

'Franck you were and always will be a legend in this Hibee's mind and I thank you for many glorious moments when you graced our club with your presence.'

Sean Allan was, for a time, joint editor of the Hibs fanzine with John Campbell. As he outlines below, Sean met Franck Sauzée at Easter Road before he had signed for Hibs or most Hibs fans even realised that he was about to join the club. He also shares his special Franck Sauzée moments.

'Saturday, 6 February 1999, was the day I first met Franck Sauzée. He and Alex Marinkov were guests of Hibs, for whom both would officially sign contracts for just four days later. I was in the hospitality suite as a guest of Alex F. Noble, the club's then car sponsor. I was lucky, too, that my good friend John Scott was with me, as it was John who recognised Franck, and we both went over to introduce ourselves, shake hands and welcome Franck Sauzée to the Hibernians.

'The 19 December 1999 is a date imprinted indelibly in the minds of many a Hibee. I am of course referring to the "Millennium" derby, but my outstanding memory of Franck Sauzée or indeed the entire match is not Franck's goal, his famous celebration or the grossly understated final score (three going on ten) but a moment of sublime skill by Franck, early in the first half.

'As fate would have it, I was once again with John Scott. We were at the match in defiance of our spouses, as were all away at Kilconquhar Castle for the weekend! Seven minutes into the game and we're under a wee bit of pressure in our own penalty area. The ball broke to Franck in the centre of the "D". Surrounded by opposition players, Franck lifted his head to look up the pitch for Russell Latapy to play the ball to. Russell was marked so, composed as ever, instead of playing the ball up field, Franck back heeled the ball towards his own goal line and straight to the toe of Shaun Dennis. Dennis was in yards of space with the time to play the ball to safety whilst keeping possession.

'Although sitting only yards away and in the heat of a much awaited derby match, my brain saw the move as if in slow motion. It was the singular, most breathtaking moment of individual skill my eyes had witnessed on a football field. Simultaneously, John and I turned our heads to face each other. No words were shared, but we both had the grins of Cheshire cats and the knowledge that this was going to be a game that Hearts never stood a chance of competing in, let alone winning. We had witnessed genius and a Hibernian legend had been born.

'My daughter Erin's first away game was Dundee Utd v Hibs on 28 October 2000. It was Hibs' first game after beating Hearts 6–2 at Easter Road; it was also Franck Sauzée's birthday. Throughout the game, the fans sang "Happy Birthday to you" to Franck. The two-year-old Erin loved this and joined in the singing. A late McManus winner made it a good day out all round. On the way home, Erin was so moved by the experience, she insisted we stop at the supermarket and buy Franck a birthday cake. The Allans celebrated Franck's birthday once again with Morrison's finest!'

Another contributor to the Hibs fanzine was Sandy Mcnair. Sandy wrote under the nom de plume 'Hibee Hippy' and was one of the magazine's most popular columnists. His most recent project is the 2011 publication *Carspotting*, which details his adventures with his close friend, fellow Hibs supporter and writer, Irvine Welsh. Sandy, too, has fond memories of the Sauzée era at Easter Road.

'Season 1998–99 was a particularly grim and in some ways shameful time to be a Hibee. Our beloved club was in the unthinkable position of playing in the First Division and I recall writing a scathing article for *Hibs Monthly*, after witnessing a wretched no-scoring draw at home to Hamilton, in which I stated that there was no way this team would bounce back to the top echelon on their current form.

'However, manager McLeish had turned the tide by Christmas and I was delighted to be (hopefully) proved wrong.

'I was even more delighted, not to say amazed, when the announcement was made that the French maestro, Franck Sauzée, was actually going to ply his trade at Easter Road! Like the George Best saga of twenty years earlier, at first I suspected a wind-up but, no, this was really happening.

'Franck was undoubtedly the biggest shock signing since Best and was, of course, another man who had held aloft European club football's most illustrious trophy. Unlike George, though, the encroaching years were never going to pose a problem for Franck fitness wise.

'My first taste of a Sauzée sizzler came in that season's 2–1 win over Falkirk courtesy of a brilliantly struck free kick. What is undoubtedly my favourite on-field Franck moment came the following season when Hibs were rightfully restored to their place at the top table. Games against our adversaries from across the city had been a ghastly endurance test under Alex Miller but that was all about to change when the Millennium Derby at the end of 1999 came round. An absolute thunderbolt from about twenty-five yards past a startled "Auntie" in the Hearts goal put Hibs two up and ensured that there was no way back for the Jambos, even though there still another half left to play.

'I was very disappointed with Franck's dismissal from his short-lived managerial role. Although understandable due to poor results, I never felt that he was given adequate time, support or backing and he was really thrust in at the deep-end right from the off.

'We have sadly seen since then that ditching managers in haste has rarely led to improvement when the next incumbent takes the hot seat. Who knows what Franck might have achieved given more time and assistance but unfortunately, this wasn't to be.

'Although Franck's tenure at Easter Road was fairly short, he will certainly never be forgotten as one of the "Alternative Famous Five" – Hibs players with European Cup winner's medals. Franck's illustrious colleagues in this select group are, of course, Ronnie Simpson, Bertie Auld, Des Bremner and George Best.

'Franck was inspirational on the park, a leader in the genuine Hibernian tradition, as exemplified in an earlier era by the great Pat Stanton. I can't think of much higher praise than that.

'Over the years, I have been honoured and privileged to have met and talked with a good few Hibernian greats. Sadly, I have never had the opportunity (not yet anyway) of meeting Franck. By all accounts he was, and no doubt still is, a really lovely bloke. A true gentleman who can consider himself as being absolutely top quality Hibernian vintage.'

Stevie Burns is also a former member of the fanzine editorial team. Stevie, too, revered Franck Sauzée. Here are his thoughts on the Gallic Great.

'Whilst for many, the memories of Franck will be the headline-grabbers – for instance, I am sure the Millennium Derby goal and subsequent celebration, and the goal in the Easter Road derby which cost him his teeth, will be covered elsewhere – personally, I most enjoyed his performances in his penultimate season at the club when he took the step back from central midfield to defence. As a centre-half myself of absolutely no distinction, I would watch with wonder at the master-class Franck would give as he patrolled behind Smith and Fenwick with an almost uncanny positional sense and timing in the tackle which approached perfection.

'He also had that ability, bestowed only on a few, to hang in the air and then propel the ball twenty or thirty yards forward with his head, having pulled the neck muscles back so that they seemed to strain at the shoulders. Or, on occasion, he would leap as if to head it, only to pull the ball down on his chest, sell the forward a dummy with those quick feet of his and then start an attack with a long accurate pass. He was marvellous to watch.

'It speaks volumes for Franck that a man with a relatively short career at the club can still be afforded the title of "legend". Especially when you consider that his last season lasted a mere six months, and was blighted by injury and an infamous, somewhat unfair, short spell as manager. Yet I can still end my own inadequate wee tribute to him with a memory from his time in the dugout. His only derby in charge was at Tynecastle, where it looked like we were heading for defeat until John O'Neil cracked home a late equaliser. The whole McLeod Street End rose as one to remind the gutted Hearts support, in loud acclaim, that "You'll Never Beat the Sauzée"! We let Franck know at that moment that, although things were not going well for him or the club, it had not cost him any of the affection and adoration he had been held in as a player. And, of course, is still held in to this day.'

Along with Stevie Burns, Colin Leslie co-founded *Hibs Monthly*. Colin is now a member of the editorial team on *The Scotsman* Sports

Desk. He has recently written two excellent football books. The first was a collaboration with great Welsh international Mel Charles and the second was the autobiography of that well loved, idiosyncratic goalkeeper, John Burridge. Colin is someone else who holds Franck Sauzée in the highest regard.

Here are his thoughts: 'When Alex McLeish signed Franck Sauzée, it was at the height of the "Bosman" era, which had expanded Scottish football's boundaries to a worldwide market – good, bad, indifferent. We didn't know it when Franck was signed but he fell in to none of those three categories – he, along with Russell Latapy, could comfortably be regarded as "great".

'Franck's pedigree was impeccable – an esteemed French international and European Cup winner – and it was viewed as an added bonus to Hibs supporters that he had helped put Rangers to the sword in the Champions League.

'However, you can never be sure how a player is going to perform when he is in the twilight of his career. In Franck's case, the jury was never out – they returned the best possible verdict on him immediately after watching a committed, professional and inspirational player with no intention of slowly winding down his career. The man oozed class and was clearly a winner, as he proved by playing a pivotal role in Hibs' return to the Premier League. After a couple of early hiccups in the First Division campaign, the recruitment of Sauzée and Latapy helped Hibs win the championship by a country mile.

'The Premier League only served to further showcase the talents of Sauzée. He was a leader and great captain for Hibs, best illustrated by his man of the match performance in a memorable 3–1 win against Hearts – losing four of his teeth in the process of scoring the second goal. It is still talked about to this day. What people often don't give Franck credit for was his hard streak. He was gentle and engaging off the pitch, had the silkiest of touches on the pitch, but yet when he needed to rise to a physical battle, he was never found wanting. The back-post header he scored against Hearts was the ultimate in bravery – he knew he would be injured in the process but didn't shirk the challenge, and even managed to shake the referee's hand in a show of respect after insisting he would carry on for the remainder of the game after being treated by the physio.

'Sauzée never shirked the job of stepping up to manage Hibs either when Alex McLeish left a team no longer firing on all cylinders to go to Rangers. It was a dirty job at that time but someone had to do it. Even Franck and all of his charisma could not lift morale or compensate for the reduction of quality in an ailing squad (although he at least managed to preserve his unbeaten derby record) and harshly the Hibs board panicked and sacked him way too soon.

'The thing that irks me most is that his abrupt departure robbed him of saying au revoir to the Hibs fans properly. He deserved a hero's send off for he was truly a Hibs hero, a man who wore the No. 4 shirt made famous by Pat Stanton well, and who I regard as my favourite Hibs player. I've seen the t-shirts with "Le God" – it's a fitting moniker. There's only one Sauzée.'

Sean McPartlin is a lifelong Hibs fan and it runs in his family. Sean's grandfather and dad supported Hibs, his uncle played for the club and his son now accompanies him to his seat in the West Stand on match days at Easter Road. As well as working as a Deputy Head Teacher in St Margaret's Academy Livingston, Sean also wrote wittily and with insight for the *Times Education Supplement Scotland*. He is rare among Hibees in that he has actually visited Franck Sauzée's hometown of Aubenas. Indeed, Sean's admiration for Leith's all-time favourite Frenchman is such that he has adopted Aubenas for his screen name on the Hibs.net website. Sean's thoughts on the superstar who is Sauzée provide evocative reading.

'The small town of Aubenas in the south-eastern region of central France is not remarkable of itself. Apart from its chateau, it has no real tourist attractions and is in many ways a typical, unaffected, French market town. When I visited it, I had no idea it was the hometown of Franck Sauzée; I was on a campsite nearby and made use of the Le Clerc supermarché on the edge of town for provisions.

'Despite its own modest bearing, Aubenas is in the midst of some of the most spectacular scenery in the whole of France. The Ardeche is famous for its rocky outcrops, with villages placed precariously on the tops, deep gorges, fast-flowing rivers and spectacular man-made and natural bridges.

'It's a dangerous place to go driving – not because of the winding mountain roads, or the ever-present pelotons of local cyclists imitating their Tour de France heroes, but because around every bend there is a heart-stopping view, another slice of natural splendour.

'And it strikes me that Aubenas is, therefore, a very suitable hometown for Sauzée. Whatever his surroundings – and in his career before Hibs, he played with some of the world's best – Franck maintained a solid, professional and unflashy demeanour. Just as unadorned Aubenas supplies the goods that maintain the spectacular tourist area that surrounds it, Franck was the Ardechois rock on which teams could be built. He had no need to show off to prove his ability, never sought to impress by being flash; he simply revealed his class by the way he played and his effect on those around him.

'His team mates improved because they played beside him, the supporters became optimistic when he led the team out, our notion of Hibernian FC as one of the world's great football clubs was burnished when Franck Sauzée talked about his love for, and understanding of, the "Eebs". Many players adopt a "rent a quote" attitude to the fans, kissing the badge, saying to the press what they feel will make them popular. Franck eschewed all that; he spoke from the heart of his love for Edinburgh and Hibs; his family, his parents and friends were all brought to Easter Road. In simple terms – Franck "got it".

'This Frenchman instinctively understood the love of Hibs that was present among the Scots, Irish, English, Asians and many others who respected the club's history and traditions, and welcomed all into the Hibernian family.

'We loved him for that. And we loved him because he was different. Not for Franck the trawl of George Street nightclubs or unfortunate press headlines. You'd be more likely to find him with his artist wife in a New Town art gallery or at the Botanics. In the summer, no Lanzarote or Florida excess: he would be fishing on the Rhone, or relaxing at his village hideaway on the Med, before returning to training, having checked his fitness with his own physician. Why couldn't Scots players have that class?

'His footballing skills, of course, even in the late stages of his career, were sublime – and when these skills combined with his love of Hibs in derby games – well, we were just delirious.

'So how will I remember this quiet Frenchman who progressed from a boyhood supporting his local boys in green at St Etienne, to a mutual love affair with the deep green of the Edinburgh Hibernians?

'The cute backheels that wrong-footed entire forward lines, the goal-scoring volleys direct from corners, the awful jig with Mixu in front of the old east stand, the blood shed scoring a derby goal, or the hundred yards dash to the away support at Tynecastle?

'Well, all of these, of course. But, strangely, the abiding picture I have of "Le God" is actually just that – a black and white picture, still available in sports photography outlets. In this picture, Franck stands in a tenement doorway on Albion Road. The collar of his leather coat is turned up and he looks every inch the hero of a French detective film – but, for all that, he seems comfortable in these somewhat mundane surroundings – no sign of this star patronising the Hibernian heartland. Behind him, slightly out of focus and time, is the Famous Five Stand, which reminds me that our other great heroes, Gordon Smith and Pat Stanton, possessed the same qualities as Franck: total professionalism, love of the club and understated influence.

'The Stand towers over the street – a symbol of the stature of our club – but it doesn't seem any taller than Franck Sauzée.'

During the writing of this book, at the author's request, John Campbell posted a thread on the Hibs.net website asking fans for their favourite Sauzée memories.

There was a marvellous response and, with apologies to those whose recollections haven't been used, a selection of the stories and views that were expressed through the thread follows. As is the custom with fans' websites, all contributors have been credited with their Hibs.net screen names.

Keith Wright Jr – 'I remember the Scottish Cup semi-final when he knocked the ball over the heads of two Livingston players. It was sheer class [Author's Note: This move is known in Argentina as the "sombrerito"]. There is no point in us ever adopting a sweeper system again as no one could ever play it like Franck.'

I Two – 'What I remember is his sheer presence and his great captaincy.'

Matty F – 'I remember a shot he took in a friendly match against Middlesbrough. It was a typical Franck rocket, which hit one defender and knocked him out. It ricocheted on to another and floored him as well. Then, of course, he never lost to Hearts did he?'

Scouse Hibee – 'I was in the Hibs shop once with my son. There was a life size cardboard cut-out of Franck Sauzée in the shop. All of a sudden, Franck stepped out from behind it and spoke to my boy, making him very happy indeed.'

Blackpool Hibs – 'It was during Franck's speech at the Franck Sauzée Appreciation Society presentation event. He broke down as he was speaking and everyone knew that they were in the presence of someone who loved Hibs and who was loved in return by all Hibs fans.'

1875er – 'In the Millennium Derby against Hearts, Franck backheeled the ball across the edge of his own box straight to Grant Brebner. He took out two Hearts players in the process.'

South Morocco Stu – 'I loved the song we used to sing to the tune of "That's Amore". It went like this, "When the ball hits the net like a low-flying jet, that's a Sauzée!"'

Hibby dog – 'I remember him doing keepie-uppies in the Scottish Cup quarter final against Falkirk.'

7 hills – 'The game after the 6–2 game was against Dundee United at Tannadice. It was the day of Franck's thirty-fifth birthday. We all sang to him, "Happy birthday to you, happy birthday to you, happy birthday Franck Sauzée, we f***ed Hearts 6–2.'

Sadtom – 'I was on a bus and Franck and his wife got on at Hanover Street. I couldn't believe my eyes when I saw this vision of loveliness appear at the top of the stairs. He was followed closely by his wife who was a bit of a looker herself.'

Cocopops 1875 – 'When Keigan Parker first broke through at St Johnstone, he was getting all the headlines and tearing teams to bits. When Hibs went to McDiarmid Park, Franck gave Parker a footballing lesson.' SixTwo added on the same theme – 'It was like watching a man having a kick about in the park with his son.'

Darlington Hibee – 'It was the day after the second leg of the UEFA Cup against AEK Athens. Franck walked past me with stitches in his swollen eye. It looked really sore. He still found the time to say, "Sorry about the result."'

Mac – 'I met him in the paper shop in Elm Row one Friday afternoon. He stood and talked to me for fifteen minutes. His passion for Hibs shone through.'

Erin go Bragh – 'At the Franck Sauzée Appreciation Society Presentation function, Franck said his gift meant more to him than winning the European Cup with Marseille. I had made my son wear a dress shirt and trousers to the event even though he hadn't been keen to do so. Franck came up to him and said, "You look very smart young man." He was made up and so was I.'

Hibsbollah – 'The life, heart and soul he gave to Hibs.'

Hi8sScottW – 'If you came home and found Franck Sauzée upstairs in bed with your wife, you would take him up a cup of tea.'

Lyonhibs – 'There was an aura about the man. He just oozed class from every pore, not to mention his undoubted qualities as a man and his love for our club.'

Stanton's Angel – 'I was at the Player of the Year presentation in the Hibs Supporters Club. A girl in our company was celebrating her eighteenth birthday. Franck brought over her birthday cake and kissed her on the cheek. He then said, "But Madame, I am a Frenchman, I have to kiss you on both cheeks." When she thanked him, he said, "I am a Hibee, too."'

Poolman – 'Just the way he said "Eeeebs!"'

Hibs 62 – 'I walked into a pub once and Franck was there. I got down on my knees and kissed his feet. I can always say that I kissed the best footballing feet at Easter Road.'

It is only fair that the group of family and friends who suggested the writing of this book should be given the opportunity to have their say (see Acknowledgements section). Nick Dishon set the ball rolling. 'Franck's presence was massive. To see him lead the team out for the Scottish Cup Final against Celtic meant everything. We knew he probably wasn't fully fit, but he was there and that made all the difference.'

Nick's cousin David added, 'He was amazingly calm and composed. He just never got flustered. It was only when Franck retired and people like Colin Murdock came in at centre back that we realised what we were missing. The only time I saw Franck lose his cool was when he kicked the dugout when he had to go off against AEK Athens.

'There was bedlam in the ground but you could still hear the noise Franck made. He was really disappointed because he knew that his leaving the field would probably cost Hibs the game and it did.'

David went on, 'The first Sauzée moment I remember was his first Hibs goal in the First Division against Morton. Russell Latapy swung a corner to Franck on the edge of the penalty area and he volleyed it sweetly into the roof of the net. I had seen Paul Scholes score a goal like that for Manchester United but I had never seen a Hibs player score a goal of that quality. It hasn't been repeated since either.'

David's dad Terry thinks that this was the moment when Hibs fans took Sauzée to their hearts. 'After that, he could do no wrong.

I remember in his last season against Kilmarnock at Easter Road, he lost the ball to Michel Ngonge, who sped away from him. Franck made as though to chase Ngonge but then, realising that he had no chance of catching him, gave a Gallic shrug and let him go. Any other player would have been crucified by the crowd for doing that but not Franck. He was beyond criticism.'

Terry's brother Michael certainly wouldn't have considered criticising Sauzée. In fact, he puts him on a pedestal. He contributed the following thoughts: 'Having first seen Hibernian play in the mid-1960s, I've seen a number of the greats. In my opinion, Franck Sauzée tops the lot. The word that sums up Franck is "grace". He had it both on the park, where I was priveleged to watch him, and off it, where I had the honour of meeting him. He clearly loved our club and shed blood for it. This adds to my regard for him. His send-off by the Franck Sauzée Appreciation Society was memorable and, to my knowledge, no other player at Hibs or any other club has been given such a farewell.'

Colin Smith reflected on Franck's time as manager. 'You couldn't say he failed because he wasn't given time to succeed. No man can master the art of management in sixty-nine days. The board should have persuaded Franck to start playing again, moved Donald Park to First Team Coach and given Franck an experienced assistant manager to support him. Think how well we played against AEK Athens. The only player from that team not at Franck's disposal was himself. If he had become a player manager, he would have made all the difference to the team and would probably never have been sacked.'

Nick Dishon had heard all about the Famous Five and Turnbull's Tornadoes but as someone who was a teenager when the Sauzée era began, he had never previously seen an outstanding Hibs team at first hand. 'I loved that team and the way it played. For the first time, I was seeing Hibs play the way I wanted them to. Franck reminded me of Franco Baresi of AC Milan when he played at the back. He was also like Lothar Matthäus and Ronald Koeman in the way he broke forward.

'Sauzée did much more in that system than just provide an extra line of cover defensively. He marshalled the players in front of him, dictating positioning and team shape and, consequently, giving tacit authority for when the wing backs were allowed to attack. He was the man with the master plan.

'What we refer to as "sweeper", the Italians call "libero", simply meaning "free". It was that freedom that allowed Sauzée to push forward to launch attacks from the centre of the park, complementing the offensive style of football we played at that time, and led to him creating and scoring more than a few goals. Eddie Turnbull once said that Russell Latapy "conducted the orchestra". He was right but Russell was only able to carry out this role because Franck had already composed the music.'

Bruce Brown, the man who had the original idea for this book, also treasured Alex McLeish's team. 'When Sauzée left, it was the end of an era. When you think how good that team was and look at the standard of our playing staff now, it is depressing. Franck called the shots and his range of passing, coupled with a knowledge of exactly what pass was required in any given situation, allowed him to fulfil a role like an American football quarterback.'

David Delaney sums up Franck's standing with a very salient point. 'Russell Latapy was an outstanding player. He was popular and classy yet when Hibs fans think back to ten years ago, they tend to talk about the "Franck Sauzée team". That shows just how special Franck was.'

Nick Dishon's father Brian, who, unlike his son, did see both the Famous Five and Turnbull's Tornadoes in action (lucky man), has his own Sauzée memory. 'It was just after the old main stand had been demolished,' recalls Brian. 'The teams changed in a portakabin and walked out to the pitch through the debris. As Franck led Hibs onto the field, the public address system was playing "Le Marseillaise". It all felt a bit surreal but that is my Franck Sauzée moment.'

The final words in this chapter go to the author's family. Kevin, the youngest member, started going to Easter Road just as Alex

Miller's period in charge was running out of steam. Next came Jocky Scott and after that Jim Duffy.

Kevin probably wondered why his mum and dad, brothers and sister got so excited about watching Hibs. When Franck Sauzée came along, he found out why. Kevin is in his twenties now and working as a primary school teacher. Here are his thoughts on the greatest living Frenchman.

'It is unusual for people in their twenties to experience nostalgia. However, that is certainly my overwhelming feeling when the name Franck Sauzée is mentioned. During harder times, people have a propensity to look back at "golden moments" in their past. For people of my age, these halcyon days will always be the time when Franck Sauzée and Russell Latapy were strutting their stuff at Easter Road.

'It was a time when free-flowing football, potent attacking play and finessed finishing were a matter of course. All flavoured with a unique blend of Franco-Caribbean style. Never before or since had Boghead seen such international flair.

'For many, there will be specific pieces of play – goals scored, passes made, moves created, which will stick in their mind and be the lasting memory of the Sauzée years. Whilst I recall many such moments – the free kick rocket against Falkirk and the howitzer against Hearts and the celebration which followed it – it is the general sense that we had a genuine footballing superstar in our midst which lingers with me.

'It seemed inconceivable that a European champion had chosen to spend the autumn of his footballing years at Easter Road. Hibees of another generation must have felt the same twenty years earlier when George Best came to play for Hibs. Best never bought into the Hibs culture the way Franck Sauzée did, though.

'I can't recall a time when people of my age felt more excited about watching Hibs. After the greyness of the Miller era and the pain of relegation, here, at last, was the palpable feeling that this team could really achieve something, perhaps even attain the Holy Grail of the Scottish Cup. That didn't happen, of course, but with Franck to inspire us, we came very close.

'Yes, there were to be darker days when Sauzée the player became Sauzée the manager but nothing will ever erase the excitement Franck created when, as a world class player, he lit up those First Division grounds and then helped Hibs soar beyond mediocrity and become the premier flair team of the Scottish Premier League.'

Kevin's brother Dominic also enjoyed the virtuoso play of Franck Sauzée, particularly his partnership with Russell Latapy. Dominic considered it a privilege to have watched these two fine players combine in the green and white of Hibernian.

'Franck Sauzée for me was synonymous with Russell Latapy. Franck and Russell, Sauzée and Latapy, their names conjure up vivid memories of a brief and exciting period in Hibs history. You could provide convincing arguments on both sides for who possessed the most talent and who had the greater influence on Hibs play. What is beyond dispute, though, is of those two wonderful footballers, only one of them gave his heart and soul to Hibernian Football club – Franck Sauzée.

'In the thirty years I have followed Hibs we have had a handful of exceptionally gifted players and many players who were consummate professionals fully committed to the Hibs cause. Franck Sauzée, in my eyes, stands alone in this era as the only player to qualify for both categories. Despite reaching the twilight of his glittering career, Franck never gave the impression he was at Easter Road to top up his pension. On the contrary, he embraced the club wholeheartedly. For his obvious passion for the club and because of the beauty of his play, the fans adored Franck. Franck always made it clear that their love was reciprocated.

'My memories of Franck are not only of his great derby performances and his majestic displays as sweeper, but of his individual pieces of skill that brought you to your feet and left you with a warm glow well after the final whistle had blown. Against Morton in the First Division, a corner was played out to Franck at the edge of the box and he volleyed it with perfect timing into the bottom corner.

'Against Celtic, he left Chris Sutton on his backside with a deft shimmy on a windy night at Easter Road. Everyone remembers his brave header against Hearts that cost him his front teeth. I remember more what followed.

'Franck broke up Hearts' next attack with a sublime back heel before dabbing his mouth with the handkerchief he still held in his hand. Frank played with style, but with a style always matched by substance.

'Unfortunately, Franck was unable to transfer his greatness from the pitch to the dugout. His early dismissal as Manager was premature and harsh but the early signs hadn't been promising. Unfortunately, the Sauzée era at Hibernian ended in sadness. Nearly ten years on, those managerial difficulties have long been forgotten but his genius as a player will live on in the hearts and minds of all Hibs fans fortunate enough to witness Franck Sauzée grace the Easter Road turf.'

Dominic's view is echoed by his sister Lisa, who doesn't even try to hide the esteem she holds Franck Sauzée in. As Lisa puts it, 'Franck Sauzée . . . the mere sound or sight of his name is enough to evoke in me instantaneous and powerful feelings of pure joy and pride. Within seconds, real time is momentarily suspended and my mind fills with a familiar but never faded series of images, which vividly transport me back to the days when I was privileged to watch this footballing genius and true gentleman in action for Hibernian. I knew then that I was in the presence of unique greatness and I savoured every magnificent move he made. I understood that I was seeing someone special lead my team.

'In my heart, though, I knew that it would only be when his playing days at Hibs were over that I would fully appreciate and reflect upon what I had witnessed. When Franck Sauzée graced the hallowed turf of Easter Road, the sun truly did shine on Leith.

'He was, is now and I strongly suspect, ever shall be, my favourite Hibs player.

'Franck Sauzée . . . Je t'adore.'

The final word goes to oldest son Patrick. Derbies mean a lot to him, as his reflections on the great Sauzée show. '"You'll love derbies," my Dad said to my brother and me as we travelled towards Tynecastle on an autumn day in 1983. "We never lose to Hearts." Well, we did that day and pretty much constantly for the rest of the 1980s and early 90s.

'Things improved slightly after Geebsie's goal broke the twenty-two game hoodoo in 1994 and Hibs gradually began to restore some self-esteem. But being honest, we still dreaded derbies and secretly felt a little inferior to our scarf-twirling Gorgie friends.

'Then came Franck. To our Gallic God, Hearts were the "wee team", just another provincial outfit. Whether playing them at Tynecastle or at ER, Franck and his co-star Russell Latapy comported themselves with all the anxiety of Hollywood Legends guesting at the Brunton Hall. Flicks, tricks and goals came in abundance. Two of the most iconic Hibs derby goals of all time were scored by Sauzée – a tracer bullet of a low shot in the Millennium Derby and a towering header that cost him four of his front teeth and Hearts another derby at Easter Road. Indeed, Hibs never lost a derby that Franck played in or managed. Memories can play tricks but in mine, Franck, highlighted in glorious green technicolor, will always slalom past monochrome maroon journeymen.

'In the build-up to another dismal derby under Bobby Williamson in November 2002, Hibs players of the past were introduced to the crowd. While all received polite applause from the home end, none elicited much response from the Jambos. Enter Pat Stanton and a crescendo of boos from the away end spoke of long submerged fear and envy of greatness. I have no doubt that Franck Sauzée would have provoked a similar response. That's how extra special he was.

'So, whilst I may never be able to tell my own little son Daniel that derbies are a doddle, I can tell him that in my experience, Hearts are nothing to fear. Franck proved it and for that, I revere him.'

The respect, admiration and affection that Hibs players and

supporters have for Franck Sauzée has come through strongly in the last two chapters. Some players are valued by their team mates but underrated by their supporters. Others are popular with the crowd but not well thought of in their dressing room. There was nothing equivocal about Sauzée's status. Those who wore green and white scarves and those fortunate enough to don the Hibs strip are united in considering Aubenas' most famous son as one of the best and best liked footballers ever to have played for Hibernian.

AUTHOR'S POSTSCRIPT

SEARCHING FOR SAUZÉE

WHEN I SET out to write this book, my intention was to create a tribute to a great Hibernian player. Franck Sauzée had arrived at Easter Road when Hibs languished in the Scottish First Division. They were probably going to get promoted but they should never have been there in the first place.

Sauzée's arrival provoked a series of emotions. There was amazement that a player of such towering reputation and achievement had agreed to come to Scotland. There was curiosity as to whether he was still capable of performing at a high level, but most of all there was delight that Hibs had captured a true European superstar.

Franck made a slow start but soon he was up and running. It was clear that he could still play and even clearer that he meant business. His joy when he scored and his obvious effort and commitment in every game sent out a strong signal. That signal spelled out the message that he was falling in love with Hibs and something special was about to unfold. Hibs supporters are as knowledgeable as they are faithful and they wasted little time in tuning into Sauzée's wavelength. They were aware that their club had signed a footballing genius who was going to have a talismanic effect upon their team.

That is exactly what happened. In the three years that followed, Franck Sauzée led Hibs into the promised land of SPL victories over Rangers, Celtic and Hearts, a Scottish Cup semi-final and final and dramatic nights in Europe. There was excitement, joy, glory and, Hibs being Hibs, a bit of disappointment along the way.

I wanted to recapture all of this, not only through my own memories but through the eyes of the players who played with and against Franck, the manager who signed him, the supporters who idolised him, the directors who appointed him as manager and then decided they had made a mistake in doing so, and the journalists and broadcasters who came to Easter Road in a professional capacity during the Sauzée era and left entranced by what they had witnessed.

In essence, my intention was to produce a personal account of three special years in the life of Hibernian Football Club. This was a time when greatness came calling down Leith way and I wanted it to be placed on record.

Although I didn't consider it essential, I had hoped to get an input from the great man himself. I wanted to meet Franck and hear what he thought of his Hibernian experience. My initial thought was that doing this wouldn't prove especially difficult. I was wrong.

It became clear very early on that Franck Sauzée is a very private man. Almost all of his former friends and colleagues had lost touch with him. None of the media people had contact details for Sauzée either.

I approached Hibs. They were most helpful. They told me that they would be delighted for Franck to return to Easter Road and take a bow on the pitch before a match. There was only one problem, though – they didn't have details of his whereabouts. Indeed, when setting up its Hall of Fame in 2010, the club had tried to get in touch with Sauzée through a number of avenues but their efforts had been in vain.

People who had been close to Franck made enquiries and put out feelers but nothing came back. Eventually, in confidence, I obtained his current address. I wrote to him and took the trouble to have the letter translated into French. I explained that the book I was writing about him was a tribute. I told him that I would like him to see it before publication so that he could reassure himself that this was the case. I gave him my telephone number, my postal address and my e-mail address. I even offered to come to France to meet him. I didn't receive a reply.

Graeme Cadger, who is chairing Ian Murray's testimonial committee, also attempted to liaise with Franck Sauzée. Ian, of course, played with Sauzée and was managed by him. Graeme made his approach through an impeccable source and invited Franck to become involved in the testimonial proceedings. He made it clear that Franck would receive five-star treatment. Like me, he drew a blank.

I had to reluctantly accept that Franck Sauzée appears to have closed the book on his time in Scottish football. He knew only success during his glittering career until he was dismissed as Hibs manager. That act hurt him deeply and it may be that he has chosen to deal with it by distancing himself from it. Ian Botham was recently interviewed about his heroic Ashes series against Australia in 1981. The interviewer asked Botham about the early part of that summer when he had struggled to score runs or take wickets before rediscovering his form so dramatically and rewriting cricketing history. The great all-rounder was direct in his answer. He said that he had blanked that all out because he didn't do failure. I suspect there is an element of this in Franck Sauzée's apparent unwillingness to re-engage with the period he spent at Easter Road.

That is a great shame. Franck is still much loved by the whole Hibernian community. If he did return to Edinburgh to reconnect with his adoring public, he would be taken aback by just how much affection for him remains. The welcome he would be given if he stepped out onto the Easter Road turf once more would be warm and wonderful. Being the emotional man he is, it would mean the world to him and, possibly, enable him to banish any bad memories that remain from the way his Hibs career ended. It would remind him of how positive an overall experience his time at Easter Road had been and allow him to return to France reliving the glories of his spell as a Hibs player and captain. That would please Franck and it would make the Hibs support happy, too. Hopefully, it will happen sooner rather than later.

In the meantime, I hope that Franck reads this book, enjoys it and feels proud of what he achieved in Scotland. I will certainly send him a copy. As he progresses through the book, he will discover, if he doesn't know already, what the Scottish football community thought of him. They considered him to be modest and polite, a man of endearing humility despite his towering gifts as a football player and the magnitude of his achievements in the game. Everybody I spoke to liked Franck Sauzée. They found him to be private but warm and friendly. He was someone more concerned with helping others and ensuring that they were given recognition for their efforts than in seeking publicity for himself. The most common response I received to the question, 'What was Franck like as a man?' was, 'Franck, oh he was a lovely man, an absolute gentleman.'

Franck Sauzée was an absolute gentleman who could play like a God when he stepped onto a football field. If I close my eyes now, I can transport myself back ten years with ease and see Franck once again in the green and white strip of the team he referred to as 'The Eebs'.

I can visualise once more the crunching tackles, the astute reading of the game that made interceptions a formality, the ability to see and execute incisive passes of both the long and short variety, the thunderous shots from dead ball kicks and open play, and the ability to leap prodigiously to meet the ball with his head.

Most of all, I can see the looks on Franck's face. The grimace of determination as he exhorted his team mates to ever greater efforts. The expression of sheer joy as he celebrated yet another goal that he had scored or created for someone else. The pain and the dejection as he lay on the turf at full time after the 2001 Scottish Cup Final at Hampden when, despite his very best efforts, Hibs had once again failed to overcome their hoodoo in this most tantalising of competitions for those who follow the Hibees. This was a man who cared passionately about Hibernian Football Club and it showed.

Well, Franck, we cared about you, too, and we still do. You lit up our club and our lives with your genius and your commitment. You gave us top quality football and reminded us that Hibs are capable of reaching the heights. We thank you for it. When you were last in Edinburgh, you received a tribute from the Franck Sauzée Appreciation Society. No one could have deserved such recognition any more than you did.

Now, ten years on, it is time for the Hibernian community to honour you again. I speak to a lot of Hibs supporters of all ages. They hold many opinions on their team – its past, its present and its future – and these views very often vary wildly. On one issue, though, they are completely united. Every Hibs fan loves Franck Sauzée. It is only one short decade since you strutted your stuff in green and white but already nostalgia has set in. When Hibs followers reflect on the 'Sauzée era', a faraway look comes into their eyes and they are transported back to a time of goals and glory. Your legend is already beyond dispute but your reputation will increase exponentially as the years roll by.

This book places on record Franck's Sauzée's impact on a football team in Leith that was in the doldrums when he arrived to play for it. By the time this great French footballer left Easter Road, Hibs had, not for the first time, risen like a phoenix from the ashes. Writing the story of Franck's years as a Hibee has been a highly pleasurable experience. I very much hope that supporters will take as much enjoyment from reading my account of that period as I gained from writing it.

It is unarguable, it is indisputable and it is an absolute fact. There's Only One Sauzée.

APPENDIX

Statistical Record of Franck Sauzee's Career Compiled by Bobby Sinnet

Franck Sauzee Hibs Career Game by Game

Season	Date			Venue	Comp	Opponent	Result	F	A	
1998-1999	Feb	20	1999	Brockville	SFL 1	Falkirk	W	2	1	
		27	1999	Somerset Park	SFL 1	Ayr United	W	3	1	
	Mar	13	1999	Boghead	SFL 1	Clydebank	L	0	2	
		20	1999	Easter Road	SFL 1	Airdrieonians	W	3	0	
	Apr	3	1999	Firhill	SFL 1	Hamilton Academical	W	2	0	
		10	1999	Stark's Park	SFL 1	Raith Rovers	W	3	1	
		17	1999	Easter Road	SFL 1	St Mirren	W	2	1	
		24	1999	Easter Road	SFL 1	Morton	W	2	1	1 Goal
	May	8	1999	Easter Road	SFL 1	Falkirk	W	2	1	1 Goal
1999-2000	July	17	1999	Koge Stadion	Friendly	Koge	D	2	2	
		20	1999	Gladsaxe Stadion	Friendly	AB	D	2	2	
		24	1999	Easter Road	Friendly	Middlesborough	W	1	0	
		31	1999	Easter Road	SPL	Motherwell	D	2	2	

Season	Date		Venue	Comp	Opponent	Result	F	A	
1999–2000	August	8	1999	Dens Park	SPL	Dundee	W	4	3	2 Goals
		14	1999	Easter Road	SPL	Heart of Midlothian	D	1	1	
		21	1999	McDairmid Park	SPL	St Johnstone	D	1	1	
		28	1999	Easter Road	SPL	Rangers	L	0	1	
	September	11	1999	Tannadice	SPL	Dundee United	L	1	3	
		19	1999	Easter Road	SPL	Kilmarnock	L	0	3	
		25	1999	Easter Road	SPL	Celtic	L	0	2	Sent Off by Referee Hugh Dallas
	October	12	1999	Rugby Park	League Cup	Kilmarnock	L	2	3	
		16	1999	Fir Park	SPL	Motherwell	D	2	2	
		23	1999	Easter Road	SPL	Dundee	W	5	2	1 Goal
		31	1999	Easter Road	SPL	Dundee United	W	3	2	
	November	6	1999	Rugby Park	SPL	Kilmarnock	W	2	0	
		20	1999	Ibrox	SPL	Rangers	L	0	2	
		24	1999	Easter Road	SPL	St Johnstone	L	0	1	First Half Substitute
		27	1999	Easter Road	SPL	Aberdeen	W	2	0	
	December	11	1999	Easter Road	SPL	Motherwell	D	2	2	
		19	1999	Tynecastle	SPL	Heart of Midlothian	W	3	0	1 Goal
		27	1999	Easter Road	SPL	Kilmarnock	D	2	2	
	January	29	2000	Easter Road	Scottish Cup	Dunfermline Athletic	W	4	1	

Month	Day	Year	Venue	Competition	Opponent	Result			Notes
February	6	2000	Easter Road	SPL	Rangers	D	2	2	
	19	2000	Easter Road	Scottish Cup	Clydebank	D	1	1	
	26	2000	Pittodrie	SPL	Aberdeen	L	0	4	
	29	2000	Cappielow	Scottish Cup	Clydebank	W	3	0	1 Goal
March	5	2000	Easter Road	SPL	Celtic	W	2	1	
	11	2000	Easter Road	Scottish Cup	Falkirk	W	3	1	
	18	2000	Easter Road	SPL	Heart of Midlothian	W	3	1	1 Goal
	25	2000	Rugby Park	SPL	Kilmarnock	L	0	1	
April	1	2000	Easter Road	SPL	Dundee United	W	1	0	
	9	2000	Hampden Park	Scottish Cup	Aberdeen	L	1	2	
	27	2000	Easter Road	SPL	Aberdeen	W	1	0	
2000-2001									
July	18	2000	Stadion am Bruchweg	Friendly	FSV Mainz	D	0	0	
	21	2000	Sportpark an Oberwald	Friendly	SV Au	W	5	0	
	30	2000	Tynecastle	SPL	Heart of Midlothian	D	0	0	
August	5	2000	Easter Road	SPL	Dundee United	W	3	0	
	12	2000	Easter Road	SPL	Dundee	W	5	1	
	16	2000	Rugby Park	SPL	Kilmarnock	W	1	0	
	19	2000	Pittodrie	SPL	Aberdeen	W	2	0	
	26	2000	Easter Road	SPL	St Mirren	W	2	0	

Season	Date		Venue	Comp	Opponent	Result	F	A	
2000-2001	September	6	2000	Brockville	League Cup	Falkirk	W	2	1	AET
	9	2000	Parkhead	SPL	Celtic	L	0	3	
	16	2000	Easter Road	SPL	Motherwell	W	2	0	
	23	2000	East End Park	SPL	Dunfermline Athletic	D	1	1	
	30	2000	McDairmid Park	SPL	St Johnstone	W	3	0	1 Goal
	October	14	2000	Easter Road	SPL	Rangers	W	1	0	
	22	2000	Easter Road	SPL	Heart of Midlothian	W	6	2	
	28	2000	Tannadice	SPL	Dundee United	W	1	0	
	November	5	2000	Dens Park	SPL	Dundee	W	2	1	
	11	2000	Easter Road	SPL	Kilmarnock	D	1	1	
	18	2000	Easter Road	SPL	Aberdeen	L	0	2	
	29	2000	Easter Road	SPL	Celtic	D	0	0	
	December	3	2000	Fir Park	SPL	Motherwell	W	3	1	
	9	2000	Easter Road	SPL	Dunfermline Athletic	W	3	0	
	16	2000	Easter Road	SPL	St Johnstone	W	2	0	
	23	2000	Ibrox	SPL	Rangers	L	0	1	
	26	2000	Tynecastle	SPL	Heart of Midlothian	D	1	1	
	30	2000	Easter Road	SPL	Dundee United	W	1	0	
	January	2	2001	Easter Road	SPL	Dundee	W	3	0	
	27	2001	Easter Road	Scottish Cup	Clyde	W	6	1	1 Goal

	Day	Year	Venue	Competition	Opponent	Result			
February	30	2001	Rugby Park	SPL	Kilmarnock	D	1	1	
	10	2001	Easter Road	SPL	St Mirren	W	4	2	1 Goal
	17	2001	Forth Bank Stadium	Scottish Cup	Stirling Albion	W	3	2	1 Goal
	25	2001	Parkhead	SPL	Celtic	D	1	1	
March	10	2001	Rugby Park	Scottish Cup	Kilmarnock	W	1	0	
April	8	2001	Easter Road	SPL	Rangers	D	0	0	
	14	2001	Hampden Park	Scottish Cup	Livingston	W	3	0	
	21	2001	Easter Road	SPL	Kilmarnock	D	1	1	
	29	2001	Dens Park	SPL	Dundee	W	2	0	
May	6	2001	Easter Road	SPL	Celtic	L	2	5	
	13	2001	Easter Road	SPL	Heart of Midlothian	D	0	0	
	20	2001	Ibrox	SPL	Rangers	L	0	4	
	26	2001	Hampden Park	Scottish Cup	Celtic	L	0	3	
2001-2002 July	14	2001	Arzon	Friendly	Olympique Marseille	W	2	1	
	17	2001	Stade du Moustoir	Friendly	FC Lorient	L	1	3	
	28	2001	Easter Road	SPL	Kilmarnock	D	2	2	1 Goal(pen)
August	4	2001	Dens Park	SPL	Dundee	L	1	2	
	11	2001	Easter Road	SPL	Aberdeen	W	2	0	1 Goal(pen)
	18	2001	Ibrox	SPL	Rangers	D	2	2	
	25	2001	Easter Road	SPL	Celtic	L	1	4	

Season	Date		Venue	Comp	Opponents	Result	F	A	
2001-2002	September	8 2001	Fir Park	SPL	Motherwell	W	3	1	2 Goals (1 pen)
		16 2001	Easter Road	SPL	Dunfermline Athletic	W	5	1	
		27 2001	Easter Road	UEFA Cup R1L2	AEK Athens	W	3	2	
	October	13 2001	Tannadice	SPL	Dundee United	L	1	3	
		21 2001	Easter Road	SPL	Heart of Midlothian	W	2	1	
		27 2001	Easter Road	SPL	Dundee	L	1	2	

FRANCK SAUZEE HIBS CAREER SUMMARY

Season	Scottish League		Scottish Cup		League Cup		UEFA Cup		Friendlies		Total	
	Apps	Goals	Apps	Goals	Apps	Goals	Apps	Goals	Apps	Goals	Apps	Goals
1998/1999	9 (0)	2	0 (0)	0	0 (0)	0	0 (0)	0	0(0)	0	9 (0)	2
1999/2000	24 (1)	5	5 (0)	1	1 (0)	0	0 (0)	0	3 (0)	0	33 (1)	6
2000/2001	33 (0)	2	5 (0)	2	1 (0)	0	0 (0)	0	2 (0)	0	41 (0)	4
2001/2002	10 (0)	4	0 (0)	0	0 (0)	0	1 (0)	0	2 (0)	0	13 (0)	4
Totals	76 (1)	13	10 (0)	3	2 (0)	0	1 (0)	0	7 (0)	0	96 (1)	16

SELECTED OTHER CAREER DETAILS

Titles

Winner of European Championship Under-21 in 1988 (France)

Winner of the European Cup in 1993 (Marseille)

Champion of France in 1989, 1990, 1992 (Marseille)

Winner of the French Cup in 1989 (Marseilles), 1991 (Monaco)

French Second Division Championship in France in 1988 (Sochaux)

French Cup Finalist in 1988 (Sochaux), 1995 (Strasbourg)

Scottish Cup Finalist in 2001 (Hibernian Edinburgh)

INTERNATIONAL DEBUT

(Paris) France – Czechoslovakia: 1-1, 24 August 1988

39 caps, 9 goals

Other teams Sochaux, Marseille, Monaco, Marseille, Atalanta, Strasbourg, Montpellier.

FRANCK SAUZEE FULL INTERNATIONAL CAREER GAME BY GAME

Season	Date			Venue	Competition	Opponent	R	F	A	
1988-1989	Aug	24	1988	Paris	Friendly	Czechoslovakia	D	1	1	
	Sep	28	1988	Paris	World Cup Qualification	Norway	W	1	0	
	Oct	22	1988	Nicosia	World Cup Qualification	Cyprus	D	1	1	
	Nov	19	1988	Belgrade	World Cup Qualification	Yugoslavia	L	2	3	1 Goal
	Feb	7	1989	Dublin	Friendly	Republic Of Ireland	D	0	0	
	Mar	8	1989	Glasgow	World Cup Qualification	Scotland	L	0	2	
	Apr	29	1989	Paris	World Cup Qualification	Yugoslavia	D	0	0	
1989-1990	Aug	16	1989	Malmo	Friendly	Sweden	W	4	2	
	Sep	5	1989	Oslo	World Cup Qualification	Norway	D	1	1	
	Oct	11	1989	Paris	World Cup Qualification	Scotland	L	0	3	
	Nov	18	1989	Toulouse	World Cup Qualification	Cyprus	W	2	0	
	Jan	21	1990	Kuwait City	Friendly	Kuwait	W	1	0	
	Jan	24	1990	Kuwait City	Friendly	East Germany	W	3	0	
	Mar	28	1990	Budapest	Friendly	Hungary	W	3	1	Captain, 1 Goal
1990-1991	Aug	15	1990	Paris	Friendly	Poland	D	0	0	Captain
	Sep	5	1990	Reykjavik	European Championship Qualifying	Iceland	W	2	1	
	Oct	13	1990	Paris	European Championship Qualifying	Czechoslovakia	W	2	1	Captain
	Nov	17	1990	Tirana	European Championship Qualifying	Albania	W	1	0	Captain
	Feb	20	1991	Paris	European Championship Qualifying	Spain	W	3	1	1 Goal
	Mar	30	1991	Paris	European Championship Qualifying	Albania	W	5	0	2 Goals

Season	Date	Year	City	Competition	Opponent	Result			Notes
1991-1992	Aug 14	1991	Poznan	Friendly	Poland	W	5	1	Captain, 1 Goal
	Sep 4	1991	Bratislava	European Championship Qualifying	Czechoslovakia	W	2	1	
	Mar 25	1992	Paris	Friendly	Belgium	D	3	3	Captain
	May 27	1992	Lausanne	Friendly	Switzerland	L	1	2	Captain
	Jun 5	1992	Lens	Friendly	Netherlands	D	1	1	Captain
	Jun 10	1992	Solna	European Championship	Sweden	D	1	1	
	Jun 14	1992	Malmo	European Championship	England	D	0	0	
1992-1993	Aug 26	1992	Paris	Friendly	Brazil	L	0	2	
	Sep 9	1992	Sofia	World Cup Qualification	Bulgaria	L	0	2	
	Oct 14	1992	Paris	World Cup Qualification	Austria	W	2	0	
	Nov 14	1992	Paris	World Cup Qualification	Finland	W	2	1	
	Feb 17	1993	Tel Aviv	World Cup Qualification	Israel	W	4	0	
	Mar 27	1993	Vienna	World Cup Qualification	Austria	W	1	0	
	Apr 28	1993	Paris	World Cup qualification	Sweden	W	2	1	Captain
	Jul 28	1993	Caen	Friendly	Russia	W	3	1	1 Goal
1993-1994	Aug 22	1993	Stockholm	World Cup Qualification	Sweden	D	1	1	1 Goal
	Sep 8	1993	Tampere	World Cup Qualification	Finland	W	2	0	1 Goal
	Oct 13	1993	Paris	World Cup Qualification	Israel	L	2	3	1 Goal
	Nov 17	1993	Paris	World Cup Qualification	Bulgaria	L	1	2